Lovingly,
Vonette Z. Bright
Matt 6:33

4.99
LR

Spring

Renew a Steadfast Spirit Within Me

VONETTE
Zachary
BRIGHT

NewLife
PUBLICATIONS

My Heart in His Hands:
Renew a Steadfast Spirit Within Me

Published by
New*Life* Publications
A ministry of Campus Crusade for Christ
P.O. Box 620877
Orlando, FL 32862-0877

Production by Genesis Group

Edited by Brenda Josee, Tammy Campbell, Joette Whims, and Lynn Copeland

Cover by Koechel Peterson Design

Printed in the United States of America

ISBN 1-56399-161-6

Unless otherwise indicated, Scripture quotations are from the *New International Version*, © 1973, 1978, 1984 by the International Bible Society. Published by Zondervan Bible Publishers, Grand Rapids, Michigan.

Scripture quotations designated Amplified are from *The Amplified Bible*, © 1965 by Zondervan Publishing House, Grand Rapids, Michigan.

For more information, write:

Campus Crusade for Christ International—100 Lake Hart Drive, Orlando, FL 32832, USA

L.I.F.E., Campus Crusade for Christ—P.O. Box 40, Flemington Markets, 2129, Australia

Campus Crusade for Christ of Canada—Box 529, Sumas, WA 98295

Campus Crusade for Christ—Fairgate House, King's Road, Tyseley, Birmingham, B11 2AA, United Kingdom

Lay Institute for Evangelism, Campus Crusade for Christ—P.O. Box 8786, Auckland, 1035, New Zealand

Campus Crusade for Christ—9 Lock Road #3-03, PacCan Centre, Singapore

Great Commission Movement of Nigeria—P.O. Box 500, Jos, Plateau State, Nigeria, West Africa

Contents

A Note of Thanks

love being a woman. My mother made womanhood seem so special. She enjoyed working in the marketplace, but in no way deprived her family. I owe my visions of womanhood to her. My desire as a Christian woman has been not only to present the gospel to all who would listen, but to encourage women to be all they can be. They do this by finding their identity in Jesus Christ and their fulfillment in His plan for their life, then exerting their influence to improve the welfare of their home, community, nation, and the world.

I believe women largely hold the moral key to society. To mobilize them for the cause of Christ, Women Today International was created. Mary Graham, a twenty-seven-year Crusade staff member, co-directed this ministry, helped launch the radio program *Women Today with Vonette Bright*, and served as its producer. The scripts for these daily programs form the basis of this book—daily nuggets to help women find answers and encouragement, cope with circumstances, and realize their significance and influence.

To extend the ministry of the radio program was a dream of Brenda Josee. She is a good friend and a great encouragement to me. Her beautiful and creative ideas have made this book a reality. She and Tammy Campbell compiled, organized, and edited the scripts, and Joette Whims and Lynn Copeland gave the material a final edit. I also thank my dear husband, Bill, my greatest source of inspiration and encouragement, with whom I have enjoyed the adventure of trusting God for over fifty years.

My heartfelt thanks go to:

The current and former staff of *Women Today*—Judy Clark, Sallie Clingman, Pam Davis, Cherry Fields, Tina Hood, Liz Lazarian, JoAnn Lynch Licht, Robin Maroudi, Patty McClung, Kathy MacLeod, Judy Nelson, Anna Patterson, Laura Staudt Sherwood, Pam Sloop, Mary Ann White, Carrie Wright; the script writers—Christy Brain, Lisa Brockman, Rebecca Cotton, Angie Bruckner Grella, Keva Harrison, Kirsten Jarrett, Roger Kemp, Cindy Kinkaid, Tracy Lambert, Christi Mansfield, Linda Wall, Kara Austin Williams, Ann Wright; "The Committee" in Orlando; The Lighthouse Report; Ambassador Advertising; Evelyn Gibson; and Jim Sanders.

All of this to say, this book has been a gift to me from the hard work of others. I now present it to you. My prayer is that these devotionals will be an encouragement to you and will help you in a greater way to entrust *your heart into His hands.*

My dear friends,

The decision is now in the hands of the jury." We understand these familiar words.

"I will take matters into my own hands." Again, we know exactly what that means. Because we take hold of things physically with our hands, our hands symbolize control of situations, emotions, and ideas.

How many times have you asked someone, "Can you handle that?" There is One who is able to perfectly handle every aspect of your life. If you have accepted the Lord Jesus Christ as your Savior, the best way to describe the security of not only this life on earth, but also the eternal destiny of your soul, is to picture *your heart in the hands of God!*

The God who promised the descendants of Abraham, "I will uphold you with my righteous right hand" (Isaiah 41:10) also holds your heart in His hands.

Life is often hectic, and the responsibilities of women in our culture place enormous demands on our physical and emotional energy. By the time we meet the needs of the day, we may find little time to seek God's heart and find solace in the strength of His hands.

I love to see a mother cradle the head of her crying newborn in her hands and gently stroke away the tears.

The security that infant feels with the familiar touch of his mother calms him to sleep. That's the scene I picture when I come to God in prayer for my own needs and express my frustrations to Him. Just sitting quietly before Him, I can sense His gentle touch caressing my aching heart, and my burden is soon lifted.

King David said it so perfectly: "You open your hand and satisfy the desires of every living thing" (Psalm 145:16).

If you have not placed your heart in His hands, please do so today. You may have accepted the Lord Jesus as your Savior but are still struggling in your life because you don't know the security, comfort, and guidance of His hand. The psalmist assures you:

He who dwells in the shelter of the Most High
will rest in the shadow of the Almighty.
I will say of the LORD, "He is my refuge and my fortress,
my God, in whom I trust." (Psalm 91:1,2)

Give Him your whole heart and experience the peace and joy that will follow you through every season of your life.

From my joyful heart to yours,

Vonette Z. Bright

Renewing Your Spirit

He put a new song in my mouth,
a hymn of praise to our God.
Many will see and fear
and put their trust in the LORD.

PSALM 40:3

The dramatic presentation of the newness in nature breaks forth each spring, reminding us once again to give thanks and praise to God for His glorious act of creation. As the bulbs that wintered deep in the soil break through the ground into spring's first flowers, our hearts fill with joy.

Springtime brings fresh new growth. It is a perfect time for us to make a new commitment to cultivate our spiritual life and experience growth.

Let's do some spiritual "spring gardening." We can dig into the fertile soil of God's Word, feeling the cool richness as it sifts through our hands. We can discover the depths of God's mercy as we examine our own heart and life and prune off the branches of indifference or discontentment.

Spend time alone with God and allow the Holy Spirit to tend the garden of your heart. You may be surprised what a little tender care from the Holy Spirit can reveal.

You will discover that the beauty of a woman wholly dedicated to God and His purpose for her life finds springtime a never-ending season. As you experience the convicting and cleansing touch of the Spirit, you will mature spiritually and release the freshness of His life in yours.

The Renewed Heart

Brothers, I do not consider myself yet to have taken hold of it. But one thing I do: Forgetting what is behind and straining toward what is ahead, I press on toward the goal to win the prize for which God has called me heavenward in Christ Jesus.

PHILIPPIANS 3:13,14

Did you know that you have a gift at your door every morning? The gift of a new day is to be treasured and used to bring glory and honor to the giver of the gift, the Lord God Almighty.

Each day brings challenges and trials that can overwhelm us and keep us from seeing the real possibilities available to us. Unfortunately, many of us carry the burdens of yesterday into our present, day after day. Jesus came to give us a life that is free of the burden of sin and filled with hope for the opportunities of a new life in Him.

Enjoying the freshness of each new day is up to you. During the times when you can't understand what God is doing, you may need to remind yourself daily of your choice to accept God's grace and receive the gift of His forgiveness.

A whispered prayer is the guarantee of a fresh start. With prayer, the beauty of life will come into clear view.

DAY 1

Some eighty years ago, Czar Nich-
olas reigned in Russia. Late in the evenings, he'd put on
a disguise and slip out into the streets of his beloved
homeland. While walking among the commoners under
his rule, he'd check on their living conditions. He'd listen to their concerns and to what was said about him.

As he passed the gate of a military base late one
night, he found the guard sound asleep. He noticed a
gun and some official financial books.

So Great a Debt

As Czar Nicholas looked closer, he realized the
guard had been embezzling money from the army.
Underneath the loaded gun was a note—apparently a
suicide note. It read: "To my horror. I decline. So great
a debt. Who can pay it?"

That night, the soldier had been overcome with
guilt about what he had done. He saw no way out of his
wrongdoing except suicide.

As the soldier woke up and reached for his gun, his
eyes were drawn to the note. There was something else
written next to his question: "Who can pay it?" He
looked closer. It read: "I, Czar Nicholas, have paid it."

Oh, dear friend, that's what God did through the death of His Son, Jesus Christ. He paid the price for our sins, canceled our debt, wiped the slate clean. He gave us forgiveness. It's as if He wrote the words "I, the Most Holy God, the Father of Jesus Christ, have paid it."

All you have to do to experience forgiveness is to repent and confess your sin. Then receive God's provision for it by placing your faith in Christ.

If you've never done so, invite Jesus Christ to come and live in your heart. Simply pray to ask Him to come in, and He will. A simple explanation of how to receive Christ through prayer is given in *Beginning Your Journey of Joy* at the back of this book.

HIS WORD
"If you confess with your mouth, 'Jesus is Lord,' and believe in your heart that God raised him from the dead, you will be saved" (Romans 10:9).

MY PART
"Merciful Lord, I praise Your name and thank You that You have paid the debt for my sin. Even though I deserve death, You have given me life. Even though I deserve the pain that You suffered, You have given me peace. Many thanks, my Lord. Amen."

MY STUDY
Psalm 51:1,2; Micah 7:18,19

DAY 2

As a single Christian in her early thirties, Kelley looked forward to the day when she would meet the right man. In the meantime, she tried to be faithful to God in every area. Kelley wanted nothing more than to please God.

Then unexpectedly, an old friend popped back into her life. They had dated for a while in college. Now ten years later, he was back and wanted to rekindle the flame.

Walk in Newness of Life

Kelley was torn. She had loved him very much. But he wasn't walking with God and had no desire to change.

On one hand, Kelley shouldn't compromise her standards for marriage. She was waiting for a man who loved God. On the other hand, she thought, "It couldn't hurt to see him now and then, could it?" So they saw each other for dinner and enjoyed a nice conversation.

Before long she had slipped back into the relationship—and not just casually. She found herself doing the things she'd promised herself she'd never do.

Unfortunately, Kelley's situation is all too common. We all get carried away with our feelings. Our guard is dropped. Lines are crossed. Sin is committed.

Kelley knew that she had a choice: either continue in a relationship that was not pleasing to God or get back on track with what she knew to be right.

The Bible says in 1 John 1:9, "If we confess our sins, he is faithful and just and will forgive us our sins and purify us from all unrighteousness."

Confession and true repentance involve turning away from our sins and walking in newness of life. Kelley decided to end the relationship, as hard as that was. Now, she is resting in the assurance that her sins are forgiven.

HIS WORD

"Blessed is he whose transgressions are forgiven, whose sins are covered" (Psalm 32:1).

MY PART

Is there an area in your life that you know is not pleasing to God? Confess it from your heart and receive God's forgiveness. Now, complete your repentance by turning from the sin. It might be difficult, but God will richly bless your obedience.

MY STUDY

1 John 1:8–10; Isaiah 55:6,7

DAY 3

Dr. Henrietta Mears, a tremendous influence in my life, told the story about a brilliant young man who was preparing to become a brain surgeon. He questioned Miss Mears about surrendering his life to God. He was convinced that becoming a Christian would mean the destruction of his personality, that he'd be altered in some strange way, and that he'd lose control of his own mind. He feared becoming a mere puppet in God's hands.

Plugged In!

So Miss Mears asked him to watch as she turned on a lamp. One moment it was dark, then she turned on the switch. She explained, "The lamp surrendered itself to the electric current and light has filled the room. The lamp didn't destroy its personality when it surrendered to the current. On the contrary—the very thing happened for which the lamp was created: it gave light."

The same would apply to other appliances—toasters, coffeepots, washing machines, vacuums. No electrical appliance is of any use until it's plugged into a source of power.

The young man got the point. He said, "If I surrender myself to God, I'll become plugged into His power.

God will illuminate my mind and fingers to make them more skillful."

That's exactly right.

People are often afraid God will step into their fireplace and put out the fire, or He'll take their violin and break all the strings. That's false! He's eager to turn your hearth into a raging fire, and He'll make beautiful music on the strings of that violin. He wants to give you a life filled with the joy of knowing with confidence that you're connected to the only Source of real power.

God has a plan for your life. It isn't for you to lose your identity or your fun. He has a wonderful plan to ensure you'll become all He created you to be.

HIS WORD
"'For I know the plans I have for you,' declares the LORD, 'plans to prosper you and not to harm you, plans to give you hope and a future'" (Jeremiah 29:11).

MY PART
"Omnipotent God, I am amazed that You have given me access to Your mighty strength. I am only a weak human vessel, but I accept the power of Your Holy Spirit who dwells in me. Help me to die to myself daily and let You work through me. Amen."

MY STUDY
Philippians 1:9; Psalm 106:8

My mother didn't want me!" the woman said. That's how Pamella's tumultuous life began. In time, drugs became her single focus to cover her pain. And selling herself was the way she got them.

But God did not give up on Pamella. When she was a child, her father's second wife took her to church. Although she heard about the God who loved her, Pamella was lost in her own painful world.

To Be Wanted

Her life plummeted. She stole liquor as a youngster, and the alcohol led to sex. As a teenager, Pamella had her first child. Eventually, she was taken in by a pimp in New York City. Pamella said, "He showed me the lights of Manhattan. And whatever he said, I did." And when she didn't, he beat her. He gave her drugs. Soon, she was prostituting for drugs. She had a second child; both children were taken in by relatives.

A crack cocaine charge landed Pamella in prison. While serving her sentence, she worked with the chaplain. "Every night, I'd write out fifty Scriptures and pass them out to other inmates," she said.

When released from prison, she was penniless and hopeless. For five years, she survived among other homeless people in the Port Authority, the city's bus terminal.

Her last dose of crack had absolutely no effect. She decided then that she'd either live or die. Crying out to God, she said, "Lord, if You'll just give me my life back…" And as is God's way, He heard the desperate cry of His dear child. He lovingly rescued Pamella and dramatically changed her life.

"I needed a chance and God gave me a chance," she said.

It wasn't easy for her to be freed from the bondage of alcohol, drugs, and sexual promiscuity, but God *never* let her go. He wanted her as His child—even when her mother didn't.

HIS WORD
"The LORD your God is with you, he is mighty to save. He will take great delight in you, he will quiet you with his love, he will rejoice over you with singing" (Zephaniah 3:17).

MY PART
"Righteous Father God, I thank you that You loved me enough to send Your Son to die for me. Thank You that You love me even when it seems no one else does. Help me to always remember how valuable I am to You. Amen."

MY STUDY
Titus 3:5,6; Psalm 27:10

ᗞAY 5

In 1979, Rusty Welborn was arrested and convicted of murder. At twenty-three years of age, he waited on death row. There he sat in a dirty, roach-infested cell.

Then he met Bob McAlister, the deputy chief of staff to South Carolina's governor. Bob was a very busy man, but one who wanted to reach out to inmates, particularly those on death row. He found Rusty.

Homecoming Day

Rusty was pitiful, unresponsive, and convinced no one cared. But that didn't stop Bob. He kept going to that filthy cell, reaching out to Rusty with the love of Christ. Bob continually reminded him that—even on death row—he could experience God's forgiveness. He kept praying for and with him.

In time, Rusty began to respond, at first tentatively and unsurely. Then one day, Rusty broke down and began to cry. That day, Rusty Welborn, a murderer, came to know Christ personally.

Bob began to see dramatic changes in him. Rusty cleaned up his cell, and he cleaned up himself!

Rusty was "amazed and thrilled" at the love of God.

To receive it freely was overwhelming and life-changing.

The day Rusty was to be executed, he told Bob, "You know, the only thing I ever wanted was a home. Now I'm going to get one." He knew he'd be entering heaven for all eternity.

That night, Bob read the Bible to him. Thinking Rusty had fallen asleep, he placed a blanket over him and kissed Rusty on the forehead. Later, as Rusty was walking to his death, he said, "What a shame that a man's gotta wait till his last night alive to be kissed and tucked in for the very first time."

Dear friend, the Lord Jesus Christ changes lives: my life, Rusty's life, your life. He also gives us unconditional love and support, things Rusty waited his entire life to receive.

HIS WORD
"I will give them an undivided heart and put a new spirit in them; I will remove from them their heart of stone and give them a heart of flesh" *(Ezekiel 11:19).*

MY PART
Is there someone you know who hasn't yet experienced the life-transforming touch of Jesus Christ? Pray for those individuals and reach out to them today. Share what Jesus has done in your life. Show them how they can receive Christ using Beginning Your Journey of Joy *or another evangelistic tract.*

MY STUDY
2 Peter 3:13,14; Psalm 84:2–4

DAY 6

Jane's early life was so dark, so abusive. Memories were stuffed below the surface of her mind where she hoped they would never appear again. But they did—nearly thirty years later.

Sexual abuse. Physical abuse. Verbal abuse. Immorality. Alcohol. These characterized Jane's childhood home life. Sin was so commonplace that she had no sense of normalcy. Before she was old enough to enter kindergarten, her innocence was stolen by her own parents and a next-door neighbor.

New Life

Jane fought back with a vengeance by becoming a model child and student. She earned straight A's and did all she could to fit into the social mainstream. No one knew that her home life was so ugly.

Then, during her high-school years, Jane suffered another violation. She was date-raped—an act no one talked about back then. Like all of her other problems, she stuffed this tragedy deep into her private world.

Jane finally came to her breaking point, blaming herself for the dark side of her life. She began drinking and using drugs. It wasn't until she lay in a hospital recovering from a drug overdose that Jane recalled what someone had told her at age fifteen: that God loved her and Jesus had given His life for her.

Jane sought out more information and ultimately gave her life to Christ, leading to an exciting period of recovery. Today her life is healthy and joyous.

Jane's life was filled with horrific circumstances and events. She had no hope. But we serve a compassionate God. He can take our sorrows, wipe them away, and give us new life through His Son. It's never too late to turn it all over to Him—the hurts, the sins, everything!

HIS WORD
"Show the wonder of your great love, you who save by your right hand those who take refuge in you from their foes"
(Psalm 17:7).

MY PART
Do you have something in your life, perhaps a pain from your past, that you still haven't turned over to God? Reflect today on this pain and give it to God in prayer. Allow Him, the Wonderful Counselor, to heal you completely. Your life will never be the same.

MY STUDY
Revelation 21:3,4; Exodus 3:7–10

DAY 7

Leonardo da Vinci's masterpiece, *The Last Supper*, has captivated millions of viewers for hundreds of years. This fifteenth-century Italian skillfully captured the facial expressions of Jesus and His disciples. There's an interesting story behind those faces. You may have heard the account, but it's worth repeating.

The Face of Forgiveness

Just as da Vinci was about to start working on *The Last Supper*, he had a bitter quarrel with a fellow painter. Leonardo was so angry and resentful that he decided to paint the face of the hated artist onto the face of Judas —the disciple who betrayed Christ. This face was one of the first he completed.

Later, when he tried to paint the face of Jesus, he lost all inspiration. No matter how hard he tried, he couldn't make any progress.

Leonardo finally realized that his mental block and loss of creativity was caused by his unresolved resentment toward his fellow artist. So he forgave the other painter, then proceeded to repaint the face of Judas so that he no longer looked like his enemy.

When he went back to work on the face of Jesus, he was inspired again. And the success of that depiction has been recognized through the centuries.

Leonardo da Vinci experienced both the bondage of anger and the freedom of resolving it. By letting go of his resentment, the destructive power of his anger was broken.

That's really what it means to forgive someone.

My friend, let me urge you to bring your emotions to God. Tell Him about the situation.

As you put into words whatever is causing your resentment, explain to God exactly how you feel. Confessing your anger opens the door for Him to heal your wounds, and enables you to exchange anger for love.

HIS WORD

"Get rid of all bitterness, rage and anger, brawling and slander, along with every form of malice. Be kind and compassionate to one another, forgiving each other, just as in Christ God forgave you" (Ephesians 4:31,32).

MY PART

Think about someone you resent. Ask God to forgive you for harboring this bitterness in your heart. Next, go to the person and ask for forgiveness. Then, let the resentment go. Move forward and remember the hurt no longer.

MY STUDY

Proverbs 25:21,22; Exodus 23:4,5

Her name is Vicki. She knows God's transforming grace firsthand. Though she had asked Jesus to be her Savior when she was young, Vicki wandered away from the truth during her college years.

It was at college that Vicki befriended an artistic group of friends. They were aspiring actors and actresses, many of whom led alternative lifestyles.

Transforming Grace

In this setting, Vicki became involved in immoral relationships and began to experiment with drugs. She hid these habits from her parents, and even tried to hide them from God.

A few years after graduating from college, Vicki was contacted by a Christian friend. She challenged Vicki to take a good look at her life and her relationship with God.

Vicki knew she had strayed from the truth and she really wanted to change. So, with the help of her friend, Vicki turned back to God.

It was a long road to recovery, but slowly and surely, Vicki allowed God to remove her bad habits. Before long, she began to use her skills for God's glory.

During the summer, she took part in a missions project—working among Navajo Indians. With her background in theatrics, Vicki helped to stage skits and plays portraying the love of Christ to junior high school students. Her creative talents were put to use, and she took delight in watching young people respond.

What a turnaround from a life of depravity! God is transforming Vicki before our very eyes.

Philippians 1:6 says, "Being confident of this, that he who began a good work in you will carry it on to completion until the day of Christ Jesus."

Just as in Vicki's life, God will be faithful in transforming your life into one that will bring glory and honor to Him.

HIS WORD

"We, who with unveiled faces all reflect the Lord's glory, are being transformed into his likeness with ever-increasing glory, which comes from the Lord, who is the Spirit" (2 Corinthians 3:18).

MY PART

"Lord Jesus, thank You for Your infinite love and boundless grace. Thank You for loving me when I am unlovable. Thank You for continuing to mold me and shape me into Your likeness. In Your precious name I pray, amen."

MY STUDY

Deuteronomy 7:6–9; Psalm 145:13,14

DAY 9

In the Book of Genesis, God said of marriage, "A man will leave his father and mother and be united to his wife, and they will become one flesh" (2:24).

Becoming one is not something that will happen in the first week of marriage or even in the first year of marriage. Becoming one is a lifetime adventure. It's a process, and it's full of both delight and difficulty!

One Flesh

Marriage is delightful because you and the one you love are now setting out on a brand new course. You're heading in the same direction, down the same path, sharing each other's dreams and desires.

On the other hand, becoming one is difficult because you and the one you love must master the art of cooperation and interdependence. At times, you both must learn to give up your own ambitions to achieve something together.

The love that you and your spouse share today can grow and become an even deeper romance and a richer experience, but only as you become one. You are not two people coming together to cheer each other on as you pursue separate goals. You are two people coming together to create a formidable team of one.

Your personality *and his*, your gifts *and his*, your interests *and his*, your desires *and his*, your goals *and his* all come together to shape a glorious picture of love. The Bible says it's the same kind of love that Christ has for His bride, the Church!

Dear friend, God will take you beyond your wildest expectations in the love He gives you for each other. All He requires is that you walk with Him and trust Him as the two of you become one. No matter how long you've been married, it's never too late to start again, to become the unique team God wants you to be.

HIS WORD
"In the Lord, however, woman is not independent of man, nor is man independent of woman. For as woman came from man, so also man is born of woman. But everything comes from God" (1 Corinthians 11:11,12).

MY PART
Thank God for your husband. Go to your husband today and tell him how much you appreciate him. If you haven't already done so, set up a time each day when you can have a devotional time together studying God's Word and praying.

MY STUDY
Mark 10:6–9; Proverbs 18:22

find that too many Christians are caught in the vicious trap of sin and guilt, sin and guilt. They know God has forgiven them, but they still keep coming back to guilt and defeat, time after time.

My friend Dr. Jack Hayford gives a wonderful illustration of this cycle.

Guilt Free

One day Pastor Jack was meeting with a young man. Bob had been deeply troubled about sin. He couldn't get victory over a recurring sin in his life. He felt like a failure as over and over he'd given in to temptation. But on this particular day he had good news to report to Dr. Hayford.

Bob said he had sinned and went, yet again, to God in prayer. While praying, the Holy Spirit taught him a profound and liberating truth. "Lord," he began praying, "I don't even feel like I deserve to come to You about this. I've failed in this way so many times. And I did it again today."

As Bob finished that prayer, he sensed the Holy Spirit whispering these words to his heart, "Did *what* again?"

Did you catch that? The Holy Spirit spoke to Bob's heart of confession and humility, and asked, "Did *what* again?"

God seemed to say to Bob, "I don't remember." It was only in that moment Bob finally understood complete forgiveness.

In Psalm 103:12, King David tells us, "As far as the east is from the west, so far has he removed our transgressions from us."

That's a distance that can't be measured. It's so far that we can't even imagine it! If God doesn't remember it, then why should we dwell on it? We need to let go of the guilt and experience God's forgiveness. Then we will experience real peace.

HIS WORD
"Then I acknowledged my sin to you, and did not cover up my iniquity . . . and you forgave the guilt of my sin" (Psalm 32:5).

MY PART
"Dear loving Lord Jesus, help me to let go of the past. You have removed my sins from Your memory. Help me to do the same so I may live in the peace of Your infinite forgiveness. Thank You for Your grace and mercy. Amen."

MY STUDY
Hebrews 8:12; Isaiah 1:18

DAY 11

Imagine giving your ten-year-old son away, having him smuggled to another country.

That's exactly what happened to little Lukas. In 1976, his Albanian parents were in despair over the repressive rule of their government. Albania was fiercely communist at the time.

Family Unity

Albania was also fiercely atheistic. The government did not allow any sign of God or symbol of Christianity within its borders.

So that year the parents of Lukas had him smuggled to America, hoping that he'd have a better life. They took a chance, not knowing if they would ever see him again.

Lukas came to live with his relatives in Des Moines, Iowa. Four years later, he heard the gospel and trusted Christ. He began to pray every day that his parents would also receive Christ.

Imagine the excitement when he returned to Albania in 1996 after communism had crumbled. He found that someone had already brought his parents the Good News, and they'd trusted Jesus Christ as their

Savior the year before his arrival. God had answered his prayers!

A team from Campus Crusade for Christ had been in this family's village. They brought the *JESUS* film, a dramatic presentation that clearly tells the story of God's love. And they stayed in the area to provide follow-up and discipleship training.

That God would bring this family together physically as well as spiritually is nothing short of a miracle. Lukas received Christ in the United States. His parents received Christ sixteen years later and half a world away, and now they will be united for eternity.

HIS WORD
"They replied, 'Believe in the Lord Jesus, and you will be saved—you and your household'" (Acts 16:31,32).

MY PART
Do you have family members who don't know Christ? Pray for them daily. Look for opportunities to share with them about the difference Jesus has made in your life. Let them see Christ in you through your kindness toward them. Love them righteously but unconditionally.

MY STUDY
Exodus 20:12; Proverbs 23:24

DAY 12

He was a preacher's kid, but in two years he earned twenty-two notches on the knife he all too often brandished. That's one notch for every time he used the knife to hurt someone.

Tom had been a model child who learned to behave as expected. In high school he was a superior student—president of the student body, the lead in school plays, member of the baseball team, and so on. But on the inside, rebellion was brewing.

A New Creation

One night he was walking down the street in Harlem when some guys jokingly asked him if he wanted to become a Harlem Lord, a gang member. Without much thought, he said, "Yes."

Tom spent several weeks causing havoc—fighting others, breaking into stores, and stealing. Then he decided to challenge the leader to a fight. Tom won, and he became gang leader for the next two years.

Amazingly, he managed to keep it a secret from his parents. He stayed active in church and school activities.

One night as Tom sat planning an attack strategy for a huge fight among several gangs, a man on the radio began talking about God. Tom didn't want to listen, but neither did he want to get up to change the station. Soon the program captured his attention. At the end of the message, Tom confessed his sin, placing his trust in Jesus Christ. His life was changed.

Though difficult, a few days later Tom showed true courage. He told 129 knife-wielding gang members about his new faith in God. In the days that followed, many of them and others from rival gangs trusted Christ. Tom later became a distinguished evangelist.

No matter what your life has been like, when you become a follower of Christ, you are made a new creation to the glory of God.

HIS WORD

"Therefore, if anyone is in Christ, he is a new creation; the old has gone, the new has come!" (2 Corinthians 5:17).

MY PART

What difference has Christ made in your life? Has He changed your attitude, actions, and how you treat others? Can you tell someone your experiences to help them know Christ personally? Practice doing that and it will make a difference in someone's life.

MY STUDY

Isaiah 64:6–8; Psalm 1:1–3

DAY 13

During the Vietnam War, a 19-year-old soldier was critically injured when a grenade exploded nearby. He lost both legs and both eyes.

For seven hours, Dr. Swan worked hard to save his life. To the surprise of many, the soldier survived.

A Life Worth Living

Noting the soldier's condition, other doctors ridiculed Dr. Swan. They chided, "He'd have been better off dead." Those harsh words haunted Dr. Swan for twenty years. Eventually he decided to find out whether his life-saving efforts had been a mistake. After a two-year search, he finally located the soldier, now a thirty-nine-year-old man.

Quite relieved, Dr. Swan was reunited with a veteran who had a strong faith in God. He had a loving family, two daughters, and a good job. Above all, this once wounded soldier had a reason for living and a spirit full of joy!

Like the soldier, many of us have been wounded in different ways—physically, emotionally, even spiritual-

---

ly. We live in a fallen world. People hurt us and we hurt others, continuing the cycle. But these hurts cannot defeat us when we place our lives in God's care. When we are feeling dejected, His arms are around us.

My friend, have you been hurt? Will you let God and His Word heal your broken heart and stitch up your wounds? God's Word is full of promises and comfort. To receive God's healing, start by memorizing the verses that speak to your need. Meditate on them. Then give God all that concerns you. In return, He will give you a life worth living.

It takes time to heal. But God can, and will, put you back on your feet. He can, and will, turn your sorrow into joy!

HIS WORD
"The LORD is close to the brokenhearted and saves those who are crushed in spirit" (Psalm 34:18).

MY PART
"Heavenly Father, You know all of my wounds and pain. I give them to You right now and ask for Your healing. Thank You for being the God of all comfort that I may come to You with everything and receive Your peace. In Your wonderful, matchless name I pray, amen."

MY STUDY
Isaiah 61:1–3; 1 Peter 4:12–16

Becky was sweet and lovely. She carried a healthy confidence in herself and a genuine love for others. One day, a friend asked Becky why she had such a good self-image.

Becky explained that it came from her mother. Her mother would hold her in her arms and, starting with her toes, say: "I love your little toes. I love your little feet. I love your little ankles. I love your little legs. I love your little thighs." And so on.

Head to Toe

Proceeding all the way up her little body, her mother named the various parts, saying: "I love your little neck …chin…mouth…nose…eyes…ears…face…hair…"

Then she'd continue, "I love you when you're good. I love you when you're bad. I love you when you're clean. I love you when you're dirty."

There was no doubt in this child's mind that she was loved. Her mother loved everything about her, and frequently told her so.

This little ritual meant so much to Becky. Even when she was twelve, she still climbed into her mother's lap and asked to hear these very same words.

Well, friend, that's how God loves you. He loves everything about you. He created you and knows every detail about you. He loves you when you're good; He loves you when you're not. His love *never* changes, no matter what. He loves you just the way you are—not like the way you wish you were. He loves you unconditionally.

He invites you to come to Him so He can demonstrate to you His love, grace, and mercy. Remember, you're loved by Him from the top of your head to the tip of your toes.

HIS WORD
"Before I formed you in the womb I knew you, before you were born I set you apart; I appointed you as a prophet to the nations" (Jeremiah 1:5).

MY PART
Tell God how thankful you are that He loves you unconditionally. How can you express to those close to you that you love them unconditionally? Start by telling them. Then demonstrate a more patient and loving attitude with them as you depend on the Holy Spirit's power. It will have a wonderful effect on them.

MY STUDY
Matthew 10:29–31; Psalm 145:15,16

Randy had talked with God, his wife, his sons, and others about moving to the inner city for a few years. A year prior to their move, Tina and Randy wondered whether they were really called to this work. They reasoned that their personalities and backgrounds didn't fit the profile of what a person would need to succeed there.

Wherever He Leads, I'll Go

Randy's an uptown kind of guy who has advanced degrees and likes opera. He could stand for an hour in front of just one painting, a strange phenomenon even among suburbanites. He wondered, "Can I learn to value, serve, befriend, and love the poorest people in the city?"

God helped the Whites see that He was bigger than all of their concerns. Their effectiveness was up to Him. As it turned out, their new neighborhood needed people with their qualities. And they have been surprised by their capacity for adapting when necessary!

In 1 Corinthians 9:22, the apostle Paul talks about intentionally becoming weak. Randy realized he could learn to talk with people with minimal education, learn to wear denims instead of slacks, learn to appreciate mariachi music, and maybe learn to eat Vietnamese food without crying.

If he tried to minister from the outside and then went home to his comfortable, insulated environment, would he really earn the credibility it would take to proclaim the gospel with authority to the inner city? He was convinced that becoming weak, as Paul said, meant living in the city and having his flower boxes stolen, seeing a car fire-bombed in the alley, experiencing gunfire on New Year's Eve, and hassling with the city to get the streetlights back on.

Reaching others for Christ may require you to go somewhere new, start over, or even become weak. Friend, don't be afraid to follow God's leading to a new and exciting adventure in life.

HIS WORD
"Be strong and take heart, all you who hope in the LORD" *(Psalm 31:24).*

MY PART
Is God calling you to a different ministry at your church or even to a new city or job? Don't be afraid. Ask God for His peace and strength. He promises to answer your prayer in a far greater way than you could imagine.

MY STUDY
1 Corinthians 9:20–22;
Isaiah 41:10

DAY 16

I am Olga. I am a communist! And will be until I die. I am an atheist! And will be until I die."

Those were the words of a 55-year-old Russian school-teacher. Staunchly, she stood to introduce herself to her discussion group.

Flesh for Stone

This was the first day of a four-day teachers' conference in Moscow, a conference about a biblically-based morals and ethics curriculum led by Americans and other Westerners. Without judgment, they demonstrated the love and acceptance of Jesus Christ to the conferees.

On day three, Olga once again stood in her discussion group. She said, "Today, I publicly denounce atheism and publicly embrace Jesus Christ as my Savior and Lord." Her heart had melted.

Nancy, one of the Americans leading the conference, said, "In one week, Olga's countenance had changed so much we didn't recognize her. It was a new Olga!"

At a party later in her home, Olga stood and again renounced communism and atheism and professed her new allegiance to Jesus Christ.

Then she revealed something remarkable. She thanked God for her two grown children who lived in Siberia, hundreds of miles from Moscow. Years earlier, they'd placed their faith in Jesus Christ. For ten years they prayed that their mother would come to Christ. Faithfully, the God of love and mercy answered their continued prayers.

Olga has grown tremendously in her faith. She prays with other Christian teachers, uses the Bible as she teaches morals and ethics, and helps more than one hundred students in a semiweekly after-school Bible study.

Pray for the Olgas in your life. Love them with God's love—with mercy, tenderness, and acceptance.

Oh, friend, reach out to your neighbors and colleagues. Spend time with them. Share His Word. Demonstrate His love. Like Olga, their hardened hearts will melt right into the hands of the Savior, Jesus Christ.

HIS WORD

"I will give you a new heart and put a new spirit in you; I will remove from you your heart of stone and give you a heart of flesh" (Ezekiel 36:26).

MY PART

Think about your neighbors and colleagues. Do they know Christ as Savior? If not, how can you help introduce them to Him? How about inviting them to a musical at your church or a Bible study? Or maybe you could ask them at an appropriate time, "If you were to die today, are you sure you would go to heaven?"

MY STUDY

2 Peter 3:9;
Psalm 86:5

In her book *A Window to Heaven*, Dr. Diane Komp tells the story of Ann and the impact her young son had on her life.

When Ann married, she gave up her nominal Christian belief, which seemed irrelevant to her new life. Although this couple was economically privileged, the romance faded early and she soon considered her marriage a disaster. But the lifestyle had its rewards, and she adored her children, especially her youngest son, T. J.

A Child Shall Lead Them

Ann never sent her children to Sunday school, and the name of God was never mentioned in their house. But one day T. J. said, "Mama, I love you more than anything in the world, except God. I love Him a little bit more!"

Stunned, she pondered, "Why would he speak of God?" Even more mysterious was why he should love a God whose name he'd never heard from her.

Two days later he followed along while his sister was horseback riding. T. J. crossed a snow-covered creek and broke through the ice. He died immediately.

The first words out of Ann's mouth when she heard the news were, "I hate you, God!" Even as she spit out the words, she felt herself held in loving arms. As her world shattered around her, she remembered that T. J. had bought her a Christmas gift that week at the Secret Santa shop at school and kept trying to give it to her. Each time he tried, she laughed and told him to put it away until Christmas. He did. After he died, she opened it. It was a beautiful necklace with a cross.

"From the mouths of babes." What an influence that little five-year-old boy had. His whole family changed. His mother experienced the true love of God in her grief. His father became a Christian. Slowly, their materialism faded away, their marriage was healed, and they became new creatures in Christ.

HIS WORD
"...and a little child will lead them" (Isaiah 11:6).

MY PART
Have you ever had a tragedy in your life? How did God turn something devastating into something good? Do you know someone going through a tragedy right now? Perhaps you could go and pray with her. Share her pain and share God's love.

MY STUDY
Luke 10:21; Psalm 8:2

DAY 18

When Becky Tirabassi surrendered her life to Christ twenty-two years ago, she changed almost instantly. She had been a self-described "morally loose, beer-drinking, bar-hopping 21-year-old." Kevin, the man she was living with and hoped to marry, was astounded that she wanted to move out, and expressed genuine concern for her emotional stability.

True Faith

She begged Kevin to consider the claims of Christ for himself. She struggled emotionally with the potential loss of one tangible love to hold onto the love of God, whom she couldn't see. Every night she cried herself to sleep, but finally realized that she had to give up on Kevin.

When she moved from California to her hometown in Ohio to develop her new relationship with God, Kevin stayed behind. They drifted apart. They eventually married other people and lost track of each other.

While visiting California recently, she was surprised to run into Kevin outside a store. Becky immediately recognized her old boyfriend and tried to get his attention. At first he didn't recognize her, but when he did, he stood stunned in the middle of the street.

Most significant to Becky about that meeting was not the reminder that she'd lost Kevin all those years ago, but that she'd gained an intimate, eternal relationship with God. Faith in God had completed her and given purpose and meaning to her once addicted, lost life. Becky has written ten books, runs her own company, been happily married to the same man for eighteen years, and reared a son.

As she says, "The transforming power of faith hinges on a relationship with the living, loving God." True faith should, will, and does change our lives and how we live. Dear friend, step out in faith and completely trust Him today. He'll do for you what He did for Becky, and me, and millions of others.

HIS WORD
"Come near to God and he will come near to you. Wash your hands, you sinners, and purify your hearts, you double-minded" (James 4:8).

MY PART
Have you ever had to say good-bye to something or someone because it wasn't pleasing to God? How has God blessed you for your faithfulness and obedience? Ask God for His guidance that you may continually be in His will.

MY STUDY
Psalm 103:1–5; Isaiah 48:17

Their fathers were ministers. They were students at a private Christian college. They were in love. And they were sexually involved.

"In the arms of this man, I thought I'd found love," Sydna said. As they pursued their relationship, the unexpected happened. Sydna became pregnant at nineteen years of age.

Forgiving the Past

"After I walked through the [clinic] doors and they told me I was pregnant, I was faced with a choice. Here I was—a boyfriend who was unsupportive, who said he'd leave me, walk away; a mother who'd been through a traumatic divorce, who I know would've been shamed; …and a baby I was carrying that I loved. Faced with these odds, stacked in this corner, I chose the one option I thought would erase my mistake. But it erased nothing."

As she walked up the steps to the abortion clinic, she sensed the Holy Spirit saying, "Don't do this." But she went on. Sydna asked the abortion counselor, "Will this affect me psychologically?"

"Oh, no," said the counselor, "it will make your problem go away; it will make your life easier."

Sydna will be the first to tell you that it was a lie. The abortion did affect her for many years, emotionally and physically. In a Bible study for women who've been through abortions, Sydna dealt with the issues in her life, discovering the assurance of God's forgiveness and learning to forgive herself.

Today, Sydna manages the Crisis Pregnancy Center Ministry of Focus on the Family. It provides resources for more than three thousand crisis pregnancy centers across the country.

Sydna encourages women to remember that there's no sin God won't forgive. However, you may need help forgiving yourself. God, through His people, will compassionately and lovingly help you deal with it.

Friend, *that's* a God of love and mercy. Turn to Him today.

HIS WORD
"I, even I, am He who blots out your transgressions, for My own sake, and remembers your sins no more" (Isaiah 43:25).

MY PART
Have you, or has someone you know, ever experienced abortion? If you have asked for forgiveness, then you are forgiven. If you are still having trouble dealing with it, seek out a good Bible-based support group. They can lovingly minister to you without condemnation. You can have peace.

MY STUDY
Psalm 85:2; Lamentations 3:22

DAY 20

Sue was struggling. She and her ex-husband were trying to reconcile their troubled marriage. Then one day, Sue met Robert and Mary.

One evening, the two couples talked for hours. Sue was so encouraged by this discussion that she asked Robert and Mary if they could help her and her ex-husband in their reconciliation.

True Hope

Robert and Mary agreed to try. But the more they learned about this couple's background, the more difficult the task seemed. Robert told them they simply had *no hope* without God!

Robert looked at the most basic need in this couple's life—their need for Christ. He shared with them the message of God's love and forgiveness. Realizing their deep sin, the struggling couple placed their trust in Christ. There they found true hope.

Today this couple is reconciled. They have put the past behind them and together are continuing to grow in the truth of God's love and forgiveness.

Friend, are you struggling? Is your marriage in trouble? Are your children rebelling? Have you lost your joy? Turn to God. As Robert said, there is "no hope without God." How true that is! Whatever circumstance you are facing, God is your only hope. Don't turn to Him when you have exhausted all other avenues of help—turn to Him *first*.

In the psalms, we read that only God can give us rest from our struggles and solid support in our distress. "Find rest, O my soul, in God alone; my hope comes from him. He alone is my rock and my salvation; he is my fortress, I will not be shaken" (62:5). What firmer foundation could we have than placing our trust in the God of the universe, who is the same yesterday, today, and forever?

HIS WORD
"But now, Lord, what do I look for? My hope is in you" (Psalm 39:7).

MY PART
Have you ever felt hopeless about a circumstance or life in general? Reflect back on that time. What gave you comfort? Perhaps that time is now. If so, ask God for His comfort and read His Word. The verses here are a good place to start.

MY STUDY
Romans 5:1–5; Jeremiah 17:7,8

Cristi packed her belongings and headed west. She was a single journalist obeying God's call to join our staff. On her U-Haul truck were her great-grandmother's wedding band, her grandfather's oak secretary, and a prized oak china cabinet she had scrimped and saved to buy. There were also photo albums, electronics, and personal items—everything she needed to set up housekeeping.

Even the Antiques

Unfortunately, the truck was stolen from the parking lot her first night in California. She moved through the first few days in shock.

Three days later, the truck was discovered in the Mojave desert a couple of hours away. But her photo albums, her bed, and some odds and ends were all that was left.

As she visited the home of some staff women a few months later, the women wanted to encourage her. They told how God had provided for them to buy a home and each item inside the home. It was quite an impressive tour. The home was beautifully furnished with antiques, and the stories of *how* God had provided

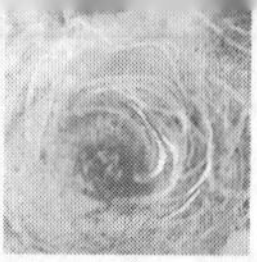

for them were overwhelming. In fact, at the end of the evening, Cristi thought to herself, "Yes, God can do that for you, but He will never do that for me."

She believed that God was *able* to do it; she just did not believe that He loved her and was *willing*. But four years later, as a newlywed, she sat in her apartment sharing with a friend how God provided for each item in her home.

Today, her home is full of antiques. She and her husband are still ministering for Christ. As guests come into her home, she tells how God provided their furnishings, giving God the glory for what He's done.

Dear friend, God loves you and wants to provide in tangible ways. Trust Him.

HIS WORD

"Now to Him who is able to do immeasurably more than all we ask or imagine according to his power that is at work within us, to him be glory" (Ephesians 3:20,21).

MY PART

"Father, the Great Provider, thank You for all that You have given me. I am constantly amazed at how much You care for my every need. Help me to continually trust You and not be concerned about the provisions of life. In Your omnipotent name I pray, amen."

MY STUDY

Psalm 34:10; Isaiah 26:3,4

All of us have sins of the past, things for which we have difficulty forgiving ourselves, let alone forgetting about. Do you hold on to sins of your past? If so, why don't you let them go? God has. The prophet Micah writes about God: "You will tread our sins underfoot and hurl all our iniquities into the depths of the sea" (7:19).

Into the Depths

Jerry Bridges, in his book *Transforming Grace*, writes about this vivid picture of God's deliberate forgiveness. He relates the picture to his own days in the Navy.

As a naval officer, he dragged grappling hooks across the bottom of the sea, looking for lost equipment. After searching all day, he realized the equipment was lost forever in the unfathomable depths of the ocean. Can you imagine losing something in such a vast place? It would be irretrievable. The same applies to our sins.

Our sins don't accidentally fall overboard. But, as Jerry says, God intentionally *hurls* "them into the depths of the sea to be lost forever, never to be recovered, never to be held against us." All because God has fully dealt with them through the death, burial, and resurrection of

His Son, Jesus Christ.

If something in your head tells you that your sins can't be forgiven, don't believe it. It is a lie from the evil one, put there to keep you from having peace and joy in your Christian walk. Instead, believe the Word of God. If Christ is your Savior and you've accepted His salvation, your sins are at the bottom of the sea, exactly where God put them.

Confess your sins today and receive His forgiveness. Then, forgive yourself. His peace awaits you.

HIS WORD
"God made him who had no sin to be sin for us, so that in him we might become the righteousness of God" (2 Corinthians 5:21).

MY PART
"Dear Lord, our Righteousness, I am amazed that You would provide salvation for a person so undeserving. That You would forgive my sins is incredible. That You would put my sins so far away from You and remember them no more is unfathomable. Thank You, Lord Jesus. Amen."

MY STUDY
Isaiah 25:9;
Psalm 68:20

DAY 23

Many of us look for love and approval in all the wrong places. We look for our identity and value in how others see us instead of how God sees us.

Pam lived in a Southern town. She was known for her deep friendships. She had a wonderful ministry, felt valued by others, and was influential for Christ. She had a secure life.

God's Sight

Then she moved away from this place of comfort. Although Pam didn't change, her environment did. Suddenly, in this new place, she no longer had the same influence or ministry. It seemed that even her questions sometimes offended people.

Throughout all this transition, Pam held fast to God and His promises. She turned to the Bible to remind herself who she was in God's sight.

In Deuteronomy 33:12, God says, "Let the beloved of the LORD rest secure in him, for he shields him all day long, and the one the LORD loves rests between his shoulders."

We are all susceptible to insecurities. We want approval and acceptance from those around us. When we don't get it, we sometimes lose our security about ourselves and our place in the world. Then we try harder to meet others' expectations of us. But the truth is, my friend, the only opinion that matters is that of the One who created us. We are the "beloved of the LORD." Can you imagine that? We have a position of importance to God Almighty!

Rest securely in the marvelous truth of His Word. Take it to heart and remind yourself of it every day. You are beloved of God and wonderfully made in His image.

HIS WORD

"You are a people holy to the LORD your God. The LORD your God has chosen you out of all the peoples on the face of the earth to be his people, his treasured possession" (Deuteronomy 7:6).

MY PART

Do you have trouble remembering how valuable you are to God? Maybe this will help you. Take some index cards and, as you read the Bible, copy down the verses that speak of God's love for you. Carry the cards with you or put them in prominent places. Read them over and over again.

MY STUDY
*John 3:16;
Psalm 34:15*

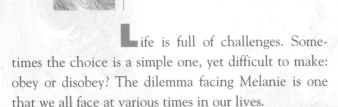

L ife is full of challenges. Sometimes the choice is a simple one, yet difficult to make: obey or disobey? The dilemma facing Melanie is one that we all face at various times in our lives.

For two years Tim and Melanie had discussed a job change that meant relocating. Although Tim sensed God's calling to go, Melanie's heart wanted to stay. Finally, she agreed to go. She didn't want to fail to obey God.

Trust and Obey

The Lord says in the Gospel of John, "If you love me, you will obey what I command" (14:15). She loved God and desired to follow His will.

Even though she had agreed to the move, the reality of the decision hit Melanie when the time came to sell their house. She burst into tears and refused to sign the contract. The thought of leaving the security of her home, friends, neighbors, and church was more than she could bear. Even though she knew that she should be obedient, the fear of change was overwhelming.

Proverbs tell us, "Whoever listens to me will live in safety and be at ease, without fear of harm" (1:33).

When we listen to God and obey His leading, His peace will be with us. There is no need to fear. This was a truth that needed to sink into Melanie's heart. It did. Finally, she chose obedience. Placing her trust in God, she signed the contract. And can you guess what happened to Tim and Melanie? God blessed their move.

Friend, is there some area where you are struggling with obedience to God—a relationship, a job, a stronghold, a gift you aren't using? Take it to Him in prayer. Be sensitive to His leading. Then obey and trust that God will bless your obedience!

HIS WORD
"Teach me to do your will, for you are my God; may your good Spirit lead me on level ground" (Psalm 143:10).

MY PART
Think about an area of your life where you feel resistant to God's leading. Are you afraid? Worried? Insecure? Read Philippians 4:13. Ask God to forgive you. Then ask Him for courage. Now, you can take the necessary steps to obey God's will.

MY STUDY
Matthew 25:20–23; Exodus 24:7

A spiritual dry spell was a bit unusual for Carol. Even though she was a Bible teacher and had frequent exposure to the Scriptures, her prayers felt like they went nowhere.

She did everything she knew to do, but she just couldn't reconnect with God. Nothing helped. Singing, praying, and reading Scripture still left her empty.

Dry Spell

Finally, in desperation, she cried out to God. There were no words, but it seemed the Spirit within was interceding for her. This was a new experience for her and a turning point in this valley of her spiritual walk. She knew that God was there.

Romans 8:26 tells us just that: "The Spirit helps us in our weakness. We do not know what we ought to pray, but the Spirit himself intercedes for us with groans that words cannot express."

Are there times when you feel the need to pray, to receive a fresh Word, infilling, or touch from God, but you don't have the words to adequately express your need? Don't fret, my friend. Instead, cry out to God. He will hear you call His name, and the Spirit will intercede for you, expressing what you cannot.

Stay in God's Word every day. The Scriptures hold answers to any and every circumstance of life and all of the emotions that go with it. Hebrews 4:12 says, "The word of God is living and active." It speaks to your needs today, just as it has to innumerable people for thousands of years.

If you are going through a dry spell like Carol did, don't give up. Keep reading the Word. Keep praying. Ask God how He would have you pray. God will meet you! He will be your turning point.

HIS WORD

"Whoever drinks the water I give him will never thirst. Indeed, the water I give him will become in him a spring of water welling up to eternal life" (John 4:14).

MY PART

"Dear loving heavenly Father, reveal to me why I lost the joy I had when I first knew You. I know that it was not just a feeling, but help me to reconnect with You so I may know Your presence, moment by moment. In Your precious name, amen."

MY STUDY

Deuteronomy 8:11–14;
Psalm 42:1–5

DAY 26

St. Augustine's influence on Christianity has been immense. His works on theology have been foundational for centuries and his autobiographical *Confessions* is a classic. Perhaps his influence is all the more powerful when you consider the struggles he had in his life.

It Is Not I

Augustine lived in fourth-century North Africa. Early in his life, he was a hot-blooded rebel who was a womanizer and a cult member. He truly lived the low life.

Even after he placed his trust in Christ, his old life continued to chase him. Occasionally, he was faced with the temptation to return to his old ways.

One day he saw an attractive female acquaintance. She invitingly called out to him, but Augustine kept walking. She kept pursuing, calling out, "Augustine! It is I! It is I!"

"Yes, I know," he replied. "But it is *not* I."

Oh, dear friend, God changes lives! Augustine became a great Christian philosopher.

Remember what the Bible says happens when you place your trust in Christ: "Therefore, if anyone is in

Christ, he is a new creation; the old has gone, the new has come!" (2 Corinthians 5:17). We are new creations, no longer slaves to what we used to do. We are "dead to sin." Although we may feel the temptation to give in to these old sins, their power over us is gone.

What is more, God has provided a way to escape the temptation of sin. "God is faithful; he will not let you be tempted beyond what you can bear. But when you are tempted, he will also provide a way out so that you can stand up under it" (1 Corinthians 10:13).

So, when you are tempted, call out to God. He *will* help you!

HIS WORD
"Because he himself suffered when he was tempted, he is able to help those who are being tempted" *(Hebrews 2:18).*

MY PART
Where is your greatest temptation? Is it coveting, lust, anger, gossip, or something else? What do you do to withstand temptation? Do you pray for strength, remove yourself from the situation, or get angry with yourself and feel defeated? Ask God for help. He will provide it.

MY STUDY
Romans 6:11–14; Psalm 119:11

DAY 27

Have you ever enjoyed that wonderful sweet camellia smell on a warm summer morning? Ahhh, that's what Mary Lou longed for! And to be warmed by Southern sunshine.

You see, God transplanted Mary Lou from the Southern U.S. to the Pacific Northwest over ten years ago. But in Oregon, the sun doesn't shine as much and camellias are hard to find! Mary Lou was homesick.

Put Down Roots

Through those years, Mary Lou refused to bury her roots. Her constant prayer was "How much longer, Lord?" She saw this as a temporary assignment until God took her back to where she longed to be.

Then one day Mary Lou saw a missions film that struck a chord in her heart. She sensed the Lord asking her, "Will you go *anywhere* for me?"

She realized her home was where the Lord led her. She decided to be content, no matter where He sent her—even Oregon!

Have you ever moved to a new place? It's tough. You have to find new friends, a new doctor, a new mechanic, a new hair stylist. That's on top of learning your way around town and adjusting to a new work environment. It can be very scary, and if you aren't careful, you will look back so fondly at the situation you came from that you won't be able to fully appreciate your new circumstance.

God said, "Never will I leave you; never will I forsake you" (Hebrews 13:5). No matter where you are, God is always with you. So don't fret, my friend. Learn to be content with where the Lord has planted you. Don't be afraid to let the roots grow. And breathe the sweet fragrance of His sovereign plan for you.

DAY 28

For two days, Houng Taing and his wife, Samoeun, had been walking. Now they were on the brink of death. They desperately needed water.

When Samoeun could go no further, she begged to stop. She cried out, "I must drink water, or I think I will die now!"

Shadow of the Almighty

They began to pray. They were only a half day from reaching freedom. They couldn't give up.

Houng prayed, "Lord Jesus, if You want us to die here, we are ready. But if You want us to live and serve You, then please show us where there is water to drink so we can go on."

Minutes later, they discovered God's provision—a hidden pool of rainwater. They rejoiced in praise to God. He renewed their strength. And late that night, they slipped across the border into Thailand, to freedom.

It was 1979, and the Taings were forced to escape their Cambodian homeland. Four years earlier, communists had taken over.

Houng and Samoeun were "guilty" of three offenses for which the communist regime was executing Cambodians. They were well-educated, had traveled abroad, and were Christians.

After the communists came to power, the Taings were in constant danger. Time and again, they turned to God in prayer. He provided, giving them shelter and protecting them. It was an extraordinarily difficult and miserable time. Death continually lurked in the shadows, but the Taings kept the faith and always trusted God.

If you have ever been in danger, did you cry out to God? Scripture gives us an emergency "911 number" to call when we are in trouble. It is Psalm 91:1, "He who dwells in the shelter of the Most High will rest in the shadow of the Almighty." We are secure in God's shadow. What safer place could we be?

HIS WORD
"The eyes of the LORD range throughout the earth to strengthen those whose hearts are fully committed to him" (2 Chronicles 16:9).

MY PART
"Our Father, Great Provider, You provide shelter for me and my family. You give us food to eat and water to drink. You clothe us and put shoes on our feet. For all of this and much more, I thank You. May Your name be praised forever. Amen."

MY STUDY
Psalm 91:1–16; Revelation 12:10–12

DAY 29

She was dearly loved by her husband. But she lived in constant fear that he'd leave her for someone else, that his love for her would die.

The fear became paralyzing, controlling. It plagued her by day and jolted her awake at night. All the while, her husband was true to her. In fact, his devotion consistently deepened. He was a wonderful provider, an encouraging counterpart, a faithful friend, and a devoted father to their seven children.

No Fear

The fear was a result of the fact that her husband had been married before, as a very young man, and had left his first wife.

Later, though, he placed his faith in Christ and God changed his life dramatically. He became a brand new person inside. When he remarried, it was for keeps. He loved God, and he loved his wife. He wanted nothing more than to be true to her. And he was.

After years of struggle with no relief, the woman received counsel from my husband. We'd been friends with this couple for years, but that conversation calmed her fears and changed her life.

First, Bill asked her to be honest with God, to tell God about her troubles and what she was feeling. Then, she must admit to God that she wasn't trusting Him. The Bible says to trust Him with *everything*. When you don't trust Him, it's a lack of faith. The Bible calls that sin.

Once she admitted her sin, she asked God to forgive her. He did. Then she thanked Him for His forgiveness and asked Him to fill her with His Holy Spirit.

As she trusted God, she was able to trust her husband. Eventually the fear subsided, and they enjoyed many years together in fruitful ministry.

My dear friend, whether you struggle with fear, doubt, or something else, learning to trust God and walk by faith is the key to life.

HIS WORD

"Trust in the LORD with all your heart and lean not on your own understanding; in all your ways acknowledge him and he will make your paths straight" (Proverbs 3:5,6).

MY PART

Reflect on your fears. Do they keep you from being all God wants you to be? Take each fear and write it down. Then search the Scriptures. There are 365 "fear nots" in the Bible— one for each day. Place a few beside each fear. Recite them. Soon you will experience victory over them.

MY STUDY

Philippians 4:6,7; Psalm 32:8–10

DAY 30

My friend Bill became a Christian when he was a student at the University of Michigan. During the early months of his Christian experience, Bill says he felt caught between two worlds. He was a smoker and carried a pack of cigarettes in his pocket. Eventually he had a desire to quit smoking, but that took a while.

Truth, Grace, and Time

Someone had given him a small pocket Bible about the size of a pack of cigarettes. When he was with his buddies at the fraternity house, he put the cigarette pack in his shirt pocket and the Bible in his hip pocket. When he was with his Christian friends, he reversed the two. One day he forgot to make the switch and found himself sheepishly explaining to his fraternity brothers why he carried a copy of the Bible!

Bill did not feel the freedom to be himself. He'd somehow gotten the message that Christians would be critical of him because he smoked.

Jesus demonstrated care and concern for people. He didn't label them. He knew that people need the truth.

But they also need grace and time. Being like Christ means loving and caring for others, accepting them, and giving them time to change.

We can choose not to be judgmental of what others do, an attitude Jesus condemned in the Pharisees. We can choose to love those who struggle with things that we do not. We can choose to accept someone whose lifestyle differs from ours. We need to fight our tendency to do anything other than this. It's through our love that others will understand the acceptance of Jesus.

People like Bill need to know they are accepted by Christ and that they're accepted by us right where they are. God is the one who creates change in the lives of others. He changed our lives. He can change anyone. It only takes His truth, His grace, and time.

HIS WORD
"Accept one another, then, just as Christ accepted you, in order to bring praise to God" (Romans 15:7).

MY PART
We don't accept sin, but we love people. Think of someone you have a hard time accepting. Now read 1 Corinthians 13:4–7. Go through each attribute of love and evaluate how it would help you accept this person. Look for opportunities to demonstrate this love. Review this practice frequently.

MY STUDY
Proverbs 17:9; Leviticus 19:18

The Nurturing Heart

Therefore, as God's chosen people, holy and
dearly loved, clothe yourselves with compassion, kindness, humility, gentleness and
patience. Bear with each other and forgive
whatever grievances you may have against one
another. Forgive as the Lord forgave you. And
over all these virtues put on love, which binds
them all together in perfect unity.

COLOSSIANS 3:12-14

The desire to nurture that God has placed within the heart of women should not be limited to the realm of children. A woman's capacity to nurture is deep and extensive. For example, studies have shown that one of the greatest attributes in female business executives is that of nurturing. Creating an environment where people can develop and lending an understanding ear and helping hand can make all the difference for co-workers or employees.

Nurturing is a process that takes time and commitment. When we fill our hearts and minds with the Word of God and His Spirit controls our lives, the impact of our nurturing can bring life-changing results.

When you have the joy of leading someone to Christ, how wonderful it is if you can also nurture or disciple your new friend as she grows in her Christian walk! You will share her excitement as she discovers the goodness of God.

Thank God for giving you the desire and ability to influence the lives of your family members, co-workers, neighbors, and friends.

When you work outside the home, achievements are measurable. You have reviews, raises, and accolades. But when you're a stay-at-home mom, sometimes your best work goes entirely unnoticed—let alone valued.

In Christ Alone

Maybe you're home with children right now, and you're missing the tangible rewards of the workplace. Perhaps you'll identify with Dee Dee, Lori, and Holly. Each of these ladies gave up her position in the work force to be a full-time mom. The transition wasn't easy.

When Dee Dee gave up an influential ministry to women, she immediately felt a sense of loss. Sure, it was wonderful to experience the joys of her first-born. But all the travel, speaking engagements, and influence came to a screeching halt when little Jeremy came along.

Lori enjoyed managing a corporate office—tackling complex accounting issues, planning marketing strategies, and motivating her staff. Her family's dual income was nearly cut in half when she decided her children needed her complete attention.

Holly managed the test kitchen for a very large food company. She invented recipes millions of people would use. You can imagine the adjustment she made in moving from the industrial kitchen to a small residential kitchen where today she tries to find something little Mark and Steven will agree to eat.

Maybe you have a similar story. It's essential for every mom to find her identity, not in her children or in her achievements, or her husband, or any other facet of life. They're all important. But it's critically important our identity comes only from Christ, who made us, loves us, and holds the key to our self-esteem.

Your work is not your life. Your home is not your life, even your children are not your life. *Christ* is your life.

Whether you're at work, at home, or managing both worlds, remember, dear friend, that your identity is found in Christ alone. Then whatever you're doing is rewarding.

HIS WORD
"For to me, to live is Christ and to die is gain" (Philippians 1:21).

MY PART
Do you ever question your decisions in life? Have you ever lost sight of your identity? Next time you do, stop, pick up the Bible, and read all the wonderful words that God wrote just for you. You are beloved of God.

MY STUDY
Exodus 15:2; Psalm 73:25,26

The Bible is filled with paradoxes, profound truths wrapped up in contrasting statements. Today, we're looking at one of the Beatitudes from the Sermon on the Mount found in Matthew 5:

Blessed are the meek, for they will inherit the earth. (v. 5)

Well, what does it mean to be meek? It sounds pretty passive, almost wimpy.

Blessed Are the Meek

Far from it!

One of the finest testimonies of contemporary meekness is from the late Corrie ten Boom. In her classic book, *The Hiding Place*, she told the amazing story about surviving World War II and the Nazi concentration camps.

At one point, she and her sister Betsy obtained a small bottle of vitamins. Since they and the other prisoners were severely malnourished, the vitamins held the key to life. In the camp, vitamins were far more valuable than gold.

Corrie's natural instinct was to hide the bottle from the others. But Betsy gently corrected her sister, saying, "If we are to be like Jesus, we should share what we have with the least of these."

So every day, Corrie opened the little bottle and dispensed the precious vitamins to the other women in their bunkhouse. Every day she worried that they would soon run out. Miraculously, the tiny bottle kept the whole bunkhouse supplied for several months!

Betsy taught Corrie and the other women in the bunkhouse the biblical principle that "meek" love is the kind that honors others enough to give away what we value most.

How about you? Do you live a life of meekness? Are you gentle in spirit?

Ask God today to help you develop this character in your life. It has rich and wonderful rewards.

HIS WORD
"Do nothing out of selfish ambition or vain conceit, but in humility consider others better than yourselves" (Philippians 2:3).

MY PART
Reflect on your life. Do you put others' needs before your own? Do you exhibit a gentle, generous spirit? Ask God to conform you to His likeness, to create a gentle spirit within you. Thank Him for His goodness.

MY STUDY
Psalm 25:8–10; Isaiah 53:7

DAY 33

Young Richard was at that awkward stage when a boy's voice changes. His face hadn't quite caught up with the growth of his nose, and he was clumsy. When he walked through the house, things broke!

One day while reaching into the fridge, he knocked over a pitcher of milk. It shattered on the floor. His pent-up frustration finally got the best of him, and he screamed, "I hate myself!"

Spilt Milk

His mother quickly wiped up the mess, wrapped her arms around him, and said, "I don't care how many pitchers of milk you spill—I love you. Everyone goes through this stage, and you *will* grow out of it, too!"

There's a lesson here for all of us. God doesn't demand perfection. He doesn't love us for how we look, what we do, or how we serve Him. He loves us as a mother loves a son or daughter—whether that person is young or old in the faith.

God doesn't stand over us with His hands on His hips, yelling. No, God will gladly clean up the mess, awaiting us with open arms.

When you accepted Christ by faith, you entered into a relationship with God that is based on His unconditional love. That means you can't do anything too terrible for Him to forgive. No mess is too big for Him to clean up.

My friend, don't get caught in the trap of trying to please God through perfection. You'll end up a very frustrated, defeated Christian.

The Christian life is not about keeping laws and trying to be a good person. No, the Christian life is recognizing your need for a Savior. You desperately need God's undying love and forgiveness.

Striving for perfection? Give yourself a break. Place all your confidence in Jesus, and in Him alone. That's the kind of woman who pleases God, and that's the kind of woman God uses.

HIS WORD
"I pray that you, being rooted and established in love, may have power, together with all the saints, to grasp how wide and long and high and deep is the love of Christ, and to know this love that surpasses knowledge" (Ephesians 3:17–19).

MY PART
"All-sufficient, loving heavenly Father, thank You for Your grace. Thank You that You love me even though I am desperately imperfect. Help me to trust only in You and not in my own abilities. Make me into the woman that You want me to be. Amen."

MY STUDY
Jeremiah 31:3; Psalm 146:5–10

DAY 34

Jealousy, nit-picking, infighting, selfish agendas—we'd like to think these problems don't occur among Christians, but we all know better! We have a lot of Kingdom work to do, but we'll crumble from within and be totally ineffective if we don't learn how to put others before ourselves.

The Habit of Encouragement

With that in mind, I'd like to offer some practical advice on encouragement, all beginning with the letter "C": compliment, confidence, and compassion.

To *compliment* a friend means to tell her what you appreciate about her. It's taking note of ways she's making progress. Not idle flattery or back-patting, but admiration founded on solid evidence. "You're great in front of an audience, Sally. People really identify with what you say." Or, "You handled that sticky situation so well, Fran! I'm learning how to lead just from watching you!"

Express *confidence* in your friends. This is especially important when someone has made a mistake.

Peter denied Christ three times. It might have been

all over—the friendship, trust, everything, but immediately after the resurrection, Jesus told Peter He still loved him and trusted him. In fact, Jesus gave Peter the enormous responsibility of caring for the rest of His followers.

Lastly, we can show *compassion*. When friends are going through hard times, they may feel unlovable. For these moments, we need to be especially supportive, to listen a lot. Instead of offering advice, we need to share in her pain, talk about our own failures, identify with her. This lets your friend know that she is not alone.

God could have selected any tool He wanted to change the world, but He chose people. We cannot function effectively unless we're working together in harmony in the home, in the office, in the church, and in our neighborhood. Let's develop the habit of encouragement. Let's stand back and be amazed at what God can do.

HIS WORD
"Do not let any unwholesome talk come out of your mouths, but only what is helpful for building others up according to their needs, that it may benefit those who listen" (Ephesians 4:29).

MY PART
Practice the art of encouragement. Observe your friends or co-workers, and look for opportunities to compliment, express confidence, and show compassion. If you do at least one of these each day, you will be amazed at the marvelous work simple kindness can do in a person's life.

MY STUDY
Proverbs 16:23,24; Ecclesiastes 4:9,10

DAY 35

A friend of mine is a popular Bible teacher. He describes the moment he realized the impact his mother had on his life and on the lives of his brother and sister.

One day he found a well-worn card above her kitchen sink. On it was a verse from Proverbs 18:

A man's gift makes room for him,
and brings him before great men. (v. 16)

Prayer Warriors

She explained that she put it there because she'd claimed the verse for all three of her children long ago. For years, she asked the Lord to use the giftedness of her children to declare His glory.

That was many years ago. Since then, his brother, Orville, has become a respected preacher and evangelist in Latin America. His sister, Luci, is a popular Christian author and speaker. And the writer of the story? Chuck Swindoll is one of the best-known and most-beloved Christian leaders in America.

That's the power of prayer! A mother's prayer. Chuck loves his mother for faithfully holding him, Orville, and Luci before the Lord in prayer throughout their lives.

Let's earn our children's respect for years to come. Let's pray for them. Nothing will have a greater impact on their lives.

The wonderful thing about prayer is that any mother can be a prayer warrior. Chuck Swindoll's mother was a homemaker who posted notes to herself around the house as reminders to pray. But if you work outside of your home, you can put prayer reminders and verses in your car or on your desk at work.

You can also pray with other mothers. All across the country, mothers are gathering in small groups for one hour each week to pray. There's real strength and encouragement to be found when you can share your concerns with other moms and leave your worries in the hands of an all-loving, all-powerful God.

HIS WORD
"Again, I tell you that if two of you on earth agree about anything you ask for, it will be done for you by my Father in heaven" (Matthew 18:19).

MY PART
Do you pray for your children, grandchildren, nieces, or nephews? How often? If you don't already have a prayer journal, start one. Keep track of the needs of these young people, pray faithfully for them, then rejoice as you write down each answer to prayer.

MY STUDY
Psalm 145:18,19; 1 Chronicles 16:8–11

DAY 36

Whenever I see young families, I am reminded of how hard it is to be young, how quickly time passes, and how important it is for our children to be nurtured—physically *and* emotionally.

Jesus demonstrated love and kindness to small children. He cared deeply about young people and gave them His undivided attention.

Personal Investment

Are you a mother who is feeling a bit weary? The responsibilities of motherhood are relentless. The work can be frustrating. Yet there's no greater priority in life than the children whom God has entrusted to you. If you feel overwhelmed, anxious, or even angry by that burden, don't be afraid to get help. Those emotions are not unusual, and someone who understands can help you know what to do. Talk to a friend, a pastor, someone you trust. We all need help with something.

Perhaps you don't have children. Maybe you think children are not your responsibility. Let me challenge that thought. As a follower of Christ, there's no room to ignore little ones. The extent of your relationships with children will vary, but be sure to seize opportunities to demonstrate kindness when you can. There are thousands of ways to make young people feel important and special. You can take a walk with a child, buy something that her school is selling, read something she's written, or listen to her reading aloud.

When you're kind to children, you're like Christ. You may even be preparing the way for a child to come to Him.

These children represent our future. Don't forget, as the chorus says, "Jesus loves the little children. All the children of the world."

HIS WORD
"Jesus said, 'Let the little children come to me, and do not hinder them, for the kingdom of heaven belongs to such as these'" (Matthew 19:14).

MY PART
Whether you have children or not, seek out opportunities to demonstrate God's love. Take an interest in the children in your neighborhood, volunteer to help in Sunday school, or ask the local school if they need help once or twice a week. Children need many positive influences. You could be one.

MY STUDY
Psalm 127:3; Proverbs 22:6

Have you ever thought about the power of listening? Let me tell you the story of Jan and Tom Schuler.

Coming back from a vacation in Florida, the Schuler's van was involved in an accident with a semi-trailer. Their daughter, Vanessa, was thrown from the vehicle and landed on her head. Little Vanessa was in a coma for three days. Two months shy of her sixth birthday, she died.

An Open Ear

It was through a neighbor that Mark and Debbie learned of this tragedy. They'd never met Jan and Tom, but they could not get them off their minds.

So Mark found the couple's telephone number and called Tom. They agreed to meet. The next week, Debbie and Jan got together as well.

In the midst of the Schuler's grieving, a deep and lasting friendship was formed. Debbie spent time with Jan, crying with her, listening, and looking at Scripture. Debbie helped Jan—who was already a Christian—to focus on God and His character as she grieved the loss of her daughter.

In the meantime, Mark gave Tom materials about

God and the Christian life. Tom had never placed his faith and trust in Christ as his Savior. Until Vanessa died, Tom thought he could handle anything. Now he felt powerless.

Mark continued to meet with Tom, listening and answering his questions about God. Within six months, Tom accepted Christ as his Savior.

The Schulers later told Mark and Debbie that they were the only ones who were willing to sit and talk. Sure, people brought meals and gave them hugs. But these new friends were the only ones who took time to go beyond the condolences. They were the only ones who listened as they struggled with deep questions about their daughter.

Make yourself available to hurting people. All it takes is an open ear and a sensitive heart. It will make all the difference!

HIS WORD

"Carry each other's burdens, and in this way you will fulfill the law of Christ" (Galatians 6:2).

MY PART

Are you a good listener to those in need? Is this an area where you could improve? Ask God to give you a sensitive heart, one that hears the emotions behind the words. The words of hurting people will take on a whole new meaning.

MY STUDY

Proverbs 17:17; Job 2:11–13

DAY 38

'm sure you know someone who's hurting, physically or emotionally. Sharon had cancer, and was told by doctors that she couldn't be cured apart from a miracle. Through her experience, she learned a lot about how to be a good friend to someone in pain.

First, take time to personally visit your hurting friend. Phone calls are great, but a knock on the door is better. If she's sick, be sure to telephone before you visit. Keep your visit to fifteen or twenty minutes unless she insists you stay longer.

Reaching Out

Second, look your friend in the eyes. And remember to smile! A smile eases tension and makes your friend feel comfortable and loved.

When your friend is giving an update on how things are going, listen carefully and give encouragement when you can. Don't gasp and say, "Oh, Sharon! Oh, dear!" Sometimes that tends to discourage people and make them think, "You know, I'm really worse off than I thought I was!"

Don't just say, "Let me know if there's anything I can do." Instead, be pro-active. Look around at what needs doing. And do it! Mow the lawn. Take out the garbage. Cook a meal. Clean the house. Baby-sit the children. Practical help lightens the burden.

When a friend is struggling, be sure to express your sadness. You don't need to have all the answers to her problems. She just needs to know you care.

Lastly, pray with your friend. Sometimes when people are hurting, they don't have the strength to pray for themselves. It can be a great comfort to hear someone else petitioning God on their behalf.

My friend, reach out in love to those who hurt. Not only will you comfort that person, you will know you're pleasing God. Nothing is more biblical or more Christlike than helping those in need.

HIS WORD
"Let us consider how we may spur one another on toward love and good deeds ...Let us encourage one another" (Hebrews 10:24,25).

MY PART
Do you know someone who has a serious illness or is going through a hard time? What can you do to help and encourage this person? Resolve to show this person in a real and practical way that God cares and that you care. Your kindness will touch them.

MY STUDY
Job 29:24; Psalm 72:12–14

DAY 39

Dr. Billy Kim of Suwon, Korea, the pastor of a ten-thousand-member Baptist church, tells this story.

Americans were on one side of the ridge, North Korean communists on the other. This was war! Bullets zipped, zoomed, and ricocheted from both zones. Many lives were lost as the ammunition often struck their targets.

Pray, Pray, Pray

This night on Heartbreak Ridge, so named by an American war correspondent, the battle was especially intense.

A bloodcurdling scream pierced the air. Fifty yards from the Americans' foxhole, in enemy territory, a young soldier was hit. In desperation, he cried out for help. Though several soldiers wanted to get to him, none dared leave the protection of the foxhole.

As time marched on, one soldier kept checking his watch. At the stroke of nine, without a word, he bravely crawled on his belly out to his wounded buddy. He grabbed him and quickly dragged him back to safety.

Later, the sergeant approached the brave soldier and asked, "Why did you wait until nine o'clock?"

The young man replied, "Sarge, when I left home my mother promised that she'd pray for me every morning at nine o'clock. I knew I'd be safe from the enemy if I went at nine o'clock."

This brave young man knew he could count on the prayers of his faithful mother. She promised to pray. He felt protected at the very moment that he knew she was asking God to keep him safe.

Do you have a child who hasn't trusted Jesus Christ, who is lost and wandering aimlessly, or who is in a dangerous circumstance?

Don't give up, my friend. God is a God who answers our prayers! Do you pray regularly for your children? Do they know you pray for them?

Today, make a commitment to pray for your children often, regularly, and without ceasing. When it counts the most, they will remember.

HIS WORD

"Pray in the Spirit on all occasions with all kinds of prayers and requests. With this in mind, be alert and always keep on praying for all the saints" (Ephesians 6:18).

MY PART

Set aside a regular time of prayer for your children. Then be sure to tell them that you consistently pray for them. Even if they don't now, one day they will be grateful for the faithful prayers of their mother.

MY STUDY

Psalm 5:1–3; Deuteronomy 7:9

DAY 40

Nancy's two little boys were terrified by sirens. Whenever they heard an ambulance or fire truck, their faces filled with fear.

One day, a screaming siren caused Nancy to pull over to the side of the road. She glanced back at the boys. They were mortified. That's when she got an idea.

She said, "Whenever we hear a siren, let's stop and thank God that someone in need is getting help. We can pretend that the siren is God calling us to pray."

Walk the Talk

The boys seemed to like the idea, so Nancy said a quick and simple prayer. For years that simple prayer has taken fear from the boys' faces.

One day she and her three-year-old, Tommy, were shopping for groceries. As they stood in the checkout line, an ambulance with flashing lights and a wailing siren pulled into the parking lot. Nancy felt a tug on her jeans.

Tommy looked up at her, "Mom! Remember?" Nancy was reluctant to pray in public. Then she thought, "Will my boys later say, 'Do you *really* believe in God, Mom? Is everything that you've told us a game? Or is it real?'"

So, she stopped for a quick prayer. In that short, simple prayer, Nancy knew she and Tommy were meeting with God right there in the checkout line of the supermarket. It was not only a statement of consistency to her child, it was also a very genuine encounter with God.

What kind of example are you to your children? Do they know you to be a woman of consistency? A woman of prayer? Teach children the appropriateness of silent prayer, but don't disappoint their expectations.

The example they see from you will influence them the rest of their lives. And nothing will have a greater influence on the world than children who love and revere God. May He richly bless you, my friend, as you invest yourself in the rearing of those precious little children.

HIS WORD
"In everything set them an example by doing what is good. In your teaching show integrity" (Titus 2:7).

MY PART
"Loving heavenly Father, thank You for the opportunity You've given me to influence these children. Help me to live a life of consistency and integrity each day so You may be glorified in their lives. Use me to show them Your ways. In Jesus' name, amen."

MY STUDY
Psalm 26:1–3; Malachi 2:5,6

DAY 41

In his book *Letters to a Young Doctor*, Dr. Richard Selzer tells of spending his Wednesday afternoons in the local library for a time of refreshing.

While there, he noticed a number of regulars, mostly elderly people. Dr. Selzer knew them only by their clothes. He named them accordingly: Old Stovepipe, Mrs. Fringes, Galoshes, and Neckerchief.

Nail Clippers and Love

One day he held the door open for Neckerchief, a stiff-walking man in his eighties. Shuffling by, Neckerchief pointed down to his knees and said, "The hinges is rusty." A wonderful friendship began.

One particular Wednesday, Dr. Selzer saw pain written all over Neckerchief's face. He asked him, "Is it the hinges?"

"Nope," Neckerchief replied. "It's the toes." He explained that his toenails had gotten too long because he couldn't reach to cut them.

Dr. Selzer left immediately to get his heavy-duty medical clippers.

When he got back, he took Neckerchief to the men's

96 | MY HEART IN HIS HANDS

room. He stooped down and took off Neckerchief's shoes and socks. He took each toe and trimmed the nail, surprisingly thick and long. It took an hour to do each foot!

Dr. Selzer did Old Stovepipe's toes the next week, Mrs. Fringes' the next. He never again went to the library without those nail clippers.

What a wonderful picture of the kind of caring attention Jesus gives, which He demonstrated by washing feet!

Think of one simple, practical thing you can do for someone else. There are so many things you and I can do to show the love of Jesus to another. Do that one thing today.

Many people share faith in action but not in words. Some share with words but show little concern by their actions. Look for ways to do both.

As you demonstrate your faith by love and service, the words you use to share your faith will be more valid.

HIS WORD
"Greater love has no one than this, that he lay down his life for his friends" (John 15:13).

MY PART
Pray that God will make you more sensitive to others' needs and observant of the little things that need to be done for someone. Take the initiative and take action. Be a humble servant, as Jesus was.

MY STUDY
Psalm 41:1;
Nehemiah 13:14

DAY 42

Dr. H. C. Morrison, a well-known minister, was walking down a busy street when he was stopped by a stranger. A man reached out and gave him a five-dollar bill.

"Thank you," the pastor said with a smile. He resumed his walk.

A few minutes later, he met a poor widow. He was aware she needed money, so he passed the five dollars along to her.

Cycle of Blessings

As Dr. Morrison went his way, he met another stranger. This person also gave him a five-dollar bill.

Soon Dr. Morrison came upon another person who also appeared needy. He said he felt strongly impressed that he should give the money to this person. This time, he decided to keep it.

Two times that day, strangers gave him unsolicited money. The first time he gave it away. The second time he kept it. No more five-dollar bills came his way that day.

He began to ponder the gifts and his response. He finally concluded, "I believe God would have continued the chain of money coming to me as I walked along if I had passed it on!"

We don't know what might have been. However, his story does illustrate a wonderful point: As he was being blessed, he became a blessing to someone else.

Giving to others doesn't necessarily mean giving money. There are thousands of things you can do to be an encouragement:

- Jot a note to your neighbor.
- Pick up a good book for a friend who's ill.
- Buy a bag of groceries for a single mom in your church.
- Call the visitors in your Sunday school class just to say hi.

The list is endless.

The next time you look in your wallet and see a five-dollar bill, think of Dr. Morrison. Let it remind you to be a blessing to someone today. It will honor God.

HIS WORD

"In everything I did, I showed you that by this kind of hard work we must help the weak, remembering the words the Lord Jesus himself said: 'It is more blessed to give than to receive'" (Acts 20:35).

MY PART

Reflect on the last time someone gave you a gift of time, money, or effort. How did you feel after receiving the gift? Blessed? Did it make you want to give also? God set it up that way. Seek out ways to give of yourself and continue the cycle of blessing.

MY STUDY

Proverbs 3:27,28; Isaiah 58:10,11

DAY 43

In a dramatic display of courage, a cat raced into a burning building to rescue her kittens, darting in and out of the burning building five times. After rescuing her kittens, she moved them, one by one, across the street—a safe distance from the fire.

With her eyes blistered shut and her paws burned, she touched each one of her offspring with her nose, making sure she'd rescued them all.

A Mother's Love

The *New York Times* article said this: "It shows with all creatures, animals or people, there's no way of measuring a mother's love."

My friend, mothers are treasures. Their love is measureless. There is no end to what a mother will do for her children. Every mother I know would run into a burning building to save her child.

I've said many times, there's no greater call than that of a mother. I can think of no other occupation with greater responsibility or greater reward.

Every day is not a burning-building kind of day, but a dedicated mother comes to the rescue in thousands of other heroic ways. She changes endless numbers of diapers, gently kisses away the pain of hundreds of stubbed

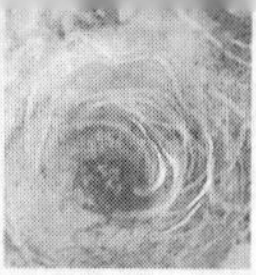

toes and scraped knees. She sacrifices lots of sleep for curfews, school projects, and children who are ill.

Your attitude toward motherhood makes a difference. Remember there are compensations at every age. Don't miss the joy of any one age. Sometimes these routine tasks may seem mundane, unrewarding, and even annoying, but they beautifully demonstrate sacrificial love —loving the way God loves.

That love is pervasive. It's all encompassing. It overrides any discomfort. It's a love that allows her to nurture and care for the child all her life, the kind of unselfish love that would drive her to run into a burning building and save her child.

Your measureless and sacrificial love will give your children more than life itself and will mark them forever, rescuing them from all kinds of situations, influencing families with God's love for generations to come.

HIS WORD

"A new command I give you: Love one another. As I have loved you, so you must love one another" (John 13:34).

MY PART

"Lord Jesus, I love because You first loved me. Thank You for the infinite love You have given me for my family. May I always hold them dear and give tirelessly to them. And may they see You in my every breath. Amen."

MY STUDY

Ruth 1:14–18; Proverbs 31:27

Not long after graduating from college, I became a Christian. I met a dear woman, Dr. Henrietta Mears.

As the Christian education director at my church, Miss Mears took me under her wing. I wanted to know more about God, what He'd done for me, how I could please Him, and how He could change my life.

Touching Lives

She was eager and thrilled with the opportunity to entrust to me all she knew about God. She taught me from God's Word, answered my questions, helped me through tough times, encouraged me, and prayed for me. She helped me grow.

Since then, God has given me the privilege of teaching others and helping them grow. I pass on to them what Miss Mears taught me. And often I hear how they're passing on to others what I've taught them.

"Discipleship" is the word used to define that kind of relationship, where one person is helping another grow in faith and become spiritually mature.

Are you in a relationship today where you're teaching what you've learned about God to someone else?

Jesus is our example. He modeled discipleship when He taught His twelve disciples how to live the Christian life and then how to teach others.

All you have to do is trust God to use you. You can start today. You don't have to know everything about God before you start. Just begin today talking with your neighbor or a friend from church about the things you know of God.

Invest your life and your love for the Lord in someone else. You'll grow and learn together.

I've seen young students do it. I've seen moms do it. I've seen professional women do it. I've seen grandmothers do it.

It's all a matter of having a willing heart. And like my friend Dr. Mears, you'll touch lives all over the world.

HIS WORD
"Pay attention and listen to the sayings of the wise; apply your heart to what I teach" (Proverbs 22:17).

MY PART
Do you know someone newer to the faith than you are? Have you considered discipling this person? Most people would welcome someone taking an active interest in their spiritual life. Ask this person if she would like to study the Bible or pray with you. You will both be blessed.

MY STUDY
John 21:15–17; Psalm 78:1–8

DAY 45

Judy was thirty-four, single, and baby-sitting four children for some friends who were out of town for the weekend. When Judy arrived at their home, there was a seven-page note waiting for her.

It read something like this:

Two children will arrive home at 2:30 and need a snack. They need to practice piano before one of them goes to soccer practice at 4:00.

Sound Investment

A neighbor will pick her up for soccer, and she will be home at 6:00. The third child will get home from her field trip at 5:30. She needs to clean her room.

The first child needs to do her chores and homework. When the second child returns from soccer, order pizza from a specific pizza place with only certain toppings. They can eat, and then pack their lunches for the next day before you pick up child four at band practice at 9 p.m. Be sure to stop and get him a hamburger on the way home.

Judy was exhausted just *reading* the instructions, much less making it happen!

Judy remembered her own mother sewing badges on her Girl Scout sash, getting her to school on time for band practice, washing her track clothes and basketball uniforms daily, driving, cooking, and then, of course, attending every event.

This is a tribute to Judy's mother and thousands like her. Thank you for all you've done to create well-rounded, happy children and for modeling Christlike servanthood.

If you're in the middle of child rearing, let me assure you it's worthwhile. At times, I'm sure, you really wonder. I did!

The time you invest in your child's life right now will reap rich rewards in the years to come. Hang in there!

God says of mothers in Proverbs 31:28, "Her children rise up and bless her. Her husband also." Today, I rise up and call you blessed. Someday your children will, too. I know, I'm there. I have two grown sons, two daughters-in-love, and four precious grandchildren. I have no regrets.

HIS WORD
"Trust in the Lord and do good . . . Commit your way to the Lord" (Psalm 37:3,5).

MY PART
"All-knowing Father God, I am in awe of Your mighty wisdom. Thank You for the blessed institution of families. Thank You for mothers. Help me each and every day to be the mother You want me to be. Amen."

MY STUDY
Proverbs 29:15; 1 Timothy 5:8

DAY 46

It was on a flight just days after the horrible plane crash in the Everglades that killed hundreds. As the flight attendants began serving a snack, a darling little eight-year-old girl preceded them. At each row, she stopped to ask every passenger, "Would you like some chips? Would you like somethin' to drink?"

Look Around

A passenger asked her what kind of juice she had. She responded, "I 'on't know." Obviously, she was new at her job!

The attendant later explained, "When she got on board in Atlanta, she was terrified. She's never flown before, and she kept talking about what happened last week in the Everglades.

"She was breathless and her speech was halting. She asked us if we'd heard about the crash. So, we decided to get her involved in helping us.

"And now, she's as happy as can be. It's as if she's forgotten all about her fear."

Being a little hostess was the best thing in the world for her.

It's a wonderful illustration of the biblical principle "It is more blessed to give than to receive." The person who gives to others focuses her attention outside herself. She's usually happier than the person who doesn't give.

Do you ever feel caught up in your own life? Living in a world of self-centeredness where *your* feelings, fears, and agendas are the most important things?

God is big enough and caring enough to meet your needs. He focuses His attention on you, so you don't have to. This frees you to lovingly reach out to others. Your attitude sweetens and time stretches. You are encouraged because God has used you.

Today, are you thinking more about yourself than others? Look around. Focus your eyes on Jesus. Ask Him to give you the strength to give to someone else. Then do it! You will receive what you could never provide for yourself—peace of mind and joy.

HIS WORD
"Learn to do right! Seek justice, encourage the oppressed. Defend the cause of the fatherless, plead the case of the widow" (Isaiah 1:17).

MY PART
"Heavenly Father, forgive me for my selfishness, for focusing on myself so much. Help me redirect my focus and reach out in service to others. Open my eyes and show me their needs so that I may show them Your love. Fill me with peace and joy. Amen."

MY STUDY
Matthew 25:34–36; Psalm 29:11

DAY 47

A little girl in England was very ill. After the doctor examined the child, he said that there was little hope she'd survive.

Like any parent, the mother tried to comfort her dying child. She quietly began talking to her precious daughter, preparing her for life beyond death's door.

Love's Embrace

"Darling," she said, "do you know you will soon hear the music of heaven? You will hear a sweeter song than you have ever heard on earth. You are very fond of music. Won't it be sweet?"

The little girl turned her head away, saying, "Oh, Momma, I am so tired and so sick that I think it would make me worse to hear all that music."

The mother then reminded her she'd soon see Jesus. "You will see the streets of heaven all paved with gold."

"Oh, Momma," the child cried out. "I am so tired I think it would make me worse to see all those beautiful things!"

Compassionately, the mother reached out to her child and gathered her up in her arms, holding her close to her heart. The little girl then whispered, "Oh,

---

Momma, this is what I want. If Jesus will only take me in His arms and let me rest!"

Oh, dear friend, I've often longed for the arms of Jesus to wrap me up, hold me tight, and let me rest! I'm sure you've felt that way yourself. Life is sometimes very difficult. We get "so tired and so sick" that we can't even enjoy the lovely things in life. But Jesus is real. He wants to hold you in His loving arms of comfort.

If you're feeling sick, tired, lonely, or discouraged, look at God's Word. Trust what He says. Let Him comfort you with His gentle Words of grace. Like the strong and caring arms of that loving mother, His arms will wrap you up and give you rest.

HIS WORD

"Cast all your anxiety on him because he cares for you" (1 Peter 5:7).

MY PART

Do you regularly feel God's loving embrace? Have you opened your heart to Him and shown Him all the hidden pain deep inside? My friend, He can make it better. Don't be afraid to let Him in. He will comfort you as no one else can. I promise.

MY STUDY

Exodus 14:13,14; Psalm 23

DAY 48

As a freshman in high school, Billy wanted desperately to play football. He practiced with the team every day. And every day Coach Mitchell would try to find a spot for Billy.

But Billy was short, overweight, and slow. He didn't look like a football player, and he couldn't run like one. His teammates nicknamed him "Turtle."

What Could Be

Billy's insightful dad talked with Coach Mitchell. He told the coach it was important to draw out the best in every player, to help them develop to their fullest potential.

Billy's dad also told the coach that he recognized Billy didn't look like a football player. But he tried to envision what his son would look like in a few years when he was a senior after Billy grew and developed with good guidance and coaching.

Then he asked, "Coach, can you see Billy with an all-American jersey covering his broad shoulders and narrow waist?"

That conversation changed Coach Mitchell. He said, "I learned to see people as they might be, not as they were or are...to see people's strengths rather than focus on their weaknesses."

In the following four years, Coach Mitchell spent extra time with Billy. All the while, he pictured him with that all-American football jersey. And you know what? By the time Billy was a senior, he'd become a star football player and an all-American!

Who's the Billy in your life? You're convinced, right now, that they'll never trust God and never amount to much.

Begin praying regularly for that person. Ask God to help you picture her as she might be when she trusts Him.

Then reach out to her and draw out her best. You'll help her develop to her fullest potential, and you'll *demonstrate* the love of Christ. As you show His love to others, He'll reveal Himself to you and to them. You'll both become all He wants you to be.

HIS WORD

"Now faith is being sure of what we hope for and certain of what we do not see" (Hebrews 11:1).

MY PART

Think of the Billy in your life. Then pray: "Lord Jesus, You created her. You have a plan for her life. Help me to see this person as You do. And may I be a positive influence on her development. Amen." Now allow God to use you.

MY STUDY

Job 8:5–7; Psalm 40:5

My good friend Doris was diagnosed with cancer. The doctors gave her a good prognosis if she had aggressive treatment. Her friends prayed. Through it all, she maintained a sense of joy and peace.

The chemotherapy worked, but the celebration was short-lived. The cancer returned, this time much worse. The doctors gave no hope for Doris.

Make an Eternal Difference

Soon Doris could no longer stay alone. Someone needed to be with her at all times. A mutual friend, Shirley, suggested her mother stay with Doris. Shirley described her mother as "cranky." And cranky she was. Her life seemed to be a series of complaints.

Doris agreed to hire Shirley's mother. What a contrast! Here was Doris, dying of cancer, maintaining a spirit of joy and trust in the Lord. And here was Shirley's mother, a picture of discontentment.

Doris began to talk to her about the Lord. She told her of His greatness, His love, His kindness, and grace. Eventually, Doris led her to faith in Christ. The joy that grew in that household was amazing. The woman's life changed dramatically.

Incredibly, during the few months she lived with Doris, she too was diagnosed with cancer. There was no treatment and no hope. Doris said, "Stay with me. We'll take care of each other." And they did.

Doris and her friend spent this time talking about life in Jesus Christ. Together they experienced the joy of the Lord, even in a desperate time of their lives.

Both women died within a month of each other. God used Doris even in her last days. God gave Doris the compassion that made an eternal difference in the life of our friend's mother.

My dear friend, God can use you. He can give you the compassion to make a difference in the life of someone else. Godly compassion will have a profound impact on your life too.

HIS WORD
"Just as the sufferings of Christ flow over into our lives, so also through Christ our comfort overflows" (2 Corinthians 1:5).

MY PART
Do you know how to lead someone to a personal relationship with Christ? It's a wonderful experience. Pick up a Beginning Your Journey of Joy *or other evangelistic piece. Read through it, keep it with you, and share with those who are open. The Holy Spirit will do the rest.*

MY STUDY
Psalm 73:23–26; Ecclesiastes 4:9–11

im was two years old and his family lived in a small apartment. His little bed was right next to his parents' bed. Frequently, his father would be awakened in the night by a little voice calling out, "Daddy? Daddy? Daddy?"

Quietly, his daddy would ask, "What Jimmy?"

"Hold my hand!" the toddler gently demanded.

Hold My Hand

His daddy would reach out in the darkness. He'd find the sweet little hand and swallow it up in his own, holding it with tender reassurance. Once safely in the grip of his big, strong daddy, Jim's arm went limp, and he began breathing deeply. Instantly, he fell soundly back to sleep.

Many years later, Jim wrote, "You see, I only wanted to know that he was there. Until the day he died, I continued to reach for him—for his assurance, for his guidance—but mostly just to know that he was there."

Jim went on to explain that when he became a father, he wanted to be like his dad. He said, "I wanted to be there for my children, a strong, warm and loving presence in their lives."

Who is little Jimmy? He is renowned child psychologist Dr. James Dobson, founder and president of Focus on the Family, a man whom God has used greatly to teach us about being loving, godly parents.

Friend, how do you love your children—with kindness, with gentleness, with fair discipline? Do you love them by showing interest in them, their joys and heartaches, their accomplishments and defeats? That's how God loves you!

That's how He wants you to love your children. Their greatest need is to be loved. Simply loved. Nothing else will ever give them greater security.

Tonight, take your child's hand in yours. Grip it with the reassuring love that only a parent can give. They'll remember it for a lifetime!

HIS WORD
"Above all else, guard your heart, for it is the wellspring of life" (Proverbs 4:23).

MY PART
Do your children know how much you love them? Do they know that you are interested in them and their lives? Take time each day to show your love by asking them how they are. Then listen for the answer. Be a "warm and loving presence" in their lives.

MY STUDY
Galatians 5:22,23; Exodus 32:31,32

DAY 51

One day while taking a test, little Rachel began daydreaming. Lost in her thoughts, her eyes roamed the classroom. She accidentally peeked at her neighbor's paper.

Rachel didn't intend to cheat, but it was too late— she decided to use her neighbor's answer as her own.

The Only Thing I Own

Later in the day, her secret began to gnaw at her conscience. Guilt set in. Very timidly, yet honestly, Rachel confessed—she told the teacher what she'd done.

Her teacher was shocked. No one in her class had ever admitted to cheating in her class. Rachel explained what she'd learned from her dad. Character, she said, is the only thing she owns. Cheating would have taken that away. It would've changed her personality, and she didn't want that to happen.

Rachel's dad, who teaches social ethics at a university, explained how he taught his daughter character. He identified two essentials: communication and leading by example.

He said, "First and foremost, parents should talk to

their children about character. Sit down with them and ask, 'Who do you want to become as a person?'

"You're not asking about what kind of job they'd like to have, but what kind of character qualities they want. Ask them what they're doing each day to help them become that kind of person."

His second response was to lead by example. Our children see everything we do. They know whether we're telling the truth or bluffing. No matter how much talking we might do, nothing replaces practicing what we preach.

Be honest with your children. Answer their questions truthfully. Then be quick to *catch* your children telling the truth and praise them for doing so. Don't just wait to catch them in a lie.

Children will make mistakes and blunders. But children of character will seek forgiveness—and in so doing, they'll stand out in the world as different.

HIS WORD
"Blessed are those who hunger and thirst for righteousness, for they will be filled" (Matthew 5:6).

MY PART
Reflect on your life as a parent. Do you live what you teach to your children? Do they see you living a life of integrity before God? None of us are perfect. Pray and ask God to help you in those problem areas. He will.

MY STUDY
Proverbs 3:1; Deuteronomy 4:9–14

DAY 52

Marilyn and her husband were rearing children, but they were also caring for an elderly parent. Eventually, they needed to place his mother in a convalescent home.

Marilyn said, "This was wrenching. Hardly a day went by without visiting her out of a sense of love coupled with guilt. Seldom did I look at the residents to the right or to the left, fearing what I saw and heard. It depressed me, and it exhausted me physically, emotionally, and spiritually."

All Together for Good

While Marilyn was visiting the nursing home, God began working it all together for good. One day Marilyn, an artist, noticed her sketchbook in the car, and sensed God prompting her to take it in with her. She began drawing a portrait of her mother-in-law.

Marilyn said, "Through art, God opened my eyes, turning my fear of the residents into love."

Marilyn's visits became longer and she began interacting with other residents. She even began drawing *their* portraits. All the while, she was talking, laughing, and even crying with them. For some, she was their only visitor. She had opportunities to share her faith in Jesus Christ, and some accepted.

She said, "Drawing their portraits gave me an entry into their lives, and relationships began to blossom. God brought blessings to me through circumstances I would never have chosen. He gave me love for the sick, hurting, disabled, and dying, and gave me a ministry within my unique circumstances."

Marilyn is an example of God's work. He knew her circumstances. He gave her a heart for the elderly. And He worked everything together for good, for Marilyn and for many, many others.

Friend, God has a plan for your life. It involves taking His love, mercy, and Word to others.

That's ministry: Making a difference for Christ in the lives of others *right where you are!*

HIS WORD
"Each one should use whatever gift he has received to serve others, faithfully administering God's grace in its various forms" (1 Peter 4:10).

MY PART
Are you in a tough circumstance right now? Ministry often comes from painful situations that God sees us through. Ask God to show you the bright side. And ask Him to show you how this situation can be turned for His glory. Get ready! God will use you.

MY STUDY
Proverbs 3:3,4;
Joshua 6:25

Several years ago while in England, Carolyn's husband had a brain tumor and was hospitalized for six months. There, Carolyn met Sophie, a tiny woman from Ghana who served tea at the hospital. Carolyn asked her if she knew Jesus, but the answer became obvious—yes!

Carolyn, an experienced discipler, suddenly found herself in the "student" role. Sophie taught her so much during those difficult days.

The Powerful

One day when Carolyn thought her husband would die, Sophie told her, "You go in and hold his hand and say, 'You belong to God.'" When the crisis passed, Sophie said, "He's better now. Didn't I tell you? Now every morning when you come in, I want you to greet the other patients and show in your face what God has done for you."

Carolyn said that at the hospital the doctors were thought to be the people with "power." But not to Sophie. She knew better. She said to Carolyn, "I pray for every patient. God heals the people."

Carolyn had always seen herself as one who could step into someone's life and help—be the wise one, the healer, the teacher. But as she observed Sophie, Carolyn changed her mind. Little Sophie, with her prayers, kind words, and cups of "hot, strong, sweet tea," was the really powerful person on the scene. She's the one who was like Jesus, bringing hope, love, and grace.

"Seeing Sophie, who did her part faithfully with joy and confidence in God, I began to pray God would make me more like her."

When we walk with God, we have the power to be used by God in another's life—no matter what our position. Let's all learn from Sophie. Pray for those around you. Bring words of hope when others are discouraged. Let the power of God be seen in you like it was in a sweet little tea lady from Ghana.

HIS WORD
"We have this treasure in jars of clay to show that this all-surpassing power is from God and not from us" (2 Corinthians 4:7).

MY PART
"Almighty God, Your awesome power is beyond measure. That You would allow me the privilege of tapping into that power is unfathomable. Through Your great love, may I be a blessing to others and a source of encouragement in their time of need. Amen."

MY STUDY
Jeremiah 32:27; Psalm 136

Barbara has six children whom she loves dearly. Like most moms, there are some tough days when she doesn't feel as patient as she'd like or everything seems to go wrong. We've all been there.

Barbara was involved in a moms' prayer group at her children's school. The moms prayed for spiritual depth in their children.

Mother's Confession

But something happened every time Barbara began praying. She said, "The Lord always brought me back to myself. I couldn't pray for spiritual awakening in our children's lives without feeling like it was an incomplete prayer—I needed spiritual renewal, too."

On the inside, Barbara was struggling with feelings of anger toward her children. She said, "I was diligent in rectifying my mistakes when I made them—for example, if I yelled at the children, or if I disciplined them out of anger, I would ask their forgiveness."

But God wanted to help her deal with the attitudes of her heart behind the anger. It was difficult, she said. She had to face the reality of her own selfishness and her desperate need for God.

As she began working through the issues, she sensed God wanted her to talk with her children about them. So one evening, the family gathered in the living room. Barbara and her husband told the children of how God had been working in their lives.

Then Barbara confessed her sinful attitudes and asked the children to forgive her. Though stunned, one by one, each child expressed their forgiveness. Today, Barbara enjoys a deeper relationship with each child. The spiritual renewal has begun in her heart and in the rest of the family.

This may seem a bit unusual, but God used the renewing of Barbara's heart to draw them all closer to each other and to Himself. She set an example of confession and forgiveness. It's a lesson they'll not likely forget.

HIS WORD
"Confess your sins to each other and pray for each other so that you may be healed" (James 5:16).

MY PART
Do you find yourself easily upset or irritated by things your children do? Ask God for forgiveness. Then go to your children to confess your sin and seek their forgiveness. Now live a life of peace and joy, a child of God because He is renewing your heart.

MY STUDY
Genesis 50:19–21; Psalm 34:22

Susan overslept. Now she would have to move like lightning. It was going to be a busy day, like so many others.

It began with getting haircuts for the children. Afterward, she took them to their grandmother's house. Then Susan dashed to a meeting, raced through the mall, and picked up a fast-food lunch.

"Will You Hug Me at Home?"

It was still early afternoon when everyone piled back into the van. On the way home, her two-year-old daughter Emily asked, "Mama, will you hug me at home?"

Susan said "Yes" to Emily's poignant question, but once at home, Susan forgot. The household chores needed to be done, and they kept her busy. Soon little Emily, fussy and cranky, became inconsolable. She was tired and needed comfort from her mom. Susan became impatient. She let her frustrations take over. In this moment, she had missed the opportunity to meet her child's need.

In 1 Corinthians 13:4,5, the Bible lays out a good

model for how we are to love: "Love is patient, love is kind…It is not easily angered, it keeps no record of wrongs." What a clear presentation of how we should treat those around us, especially our children.

My friend, I know it is hard to be a mom. We have all had those moments where everything is overwhelming—all the appointments, responsibilities, and different roles we have to play. But the most important role of a mother is to fill your children with your tender love. Slow down and take the time to hug and hold them. It exhibits God's love. This love builds security in your children. This, in turn, may even pre-empt some of those difficult moments—after all, a secure child is a happy child.

HIS WORD

"Sons are a heritage from the LORD, children a reward from him" (Psalm 127:3).

MY PART

How often do you hug your children and tell them that you love them? Children need to be reminded in tangible ways that they are loved. Make it a point each and every day to reassure your children of their place in your heart.

MY STUDY

1 John 4:12; Exodus 2:1–10

DAY 56

It was a simple childhood incident, but it left an indelible mark on Karen's heart.

One evening, the family hurriedly piled into the car to go to a party. Her mom gently said to her dad, "What a busy day! I feel like I haven't seen you in a week!" Then she suggested they look into each other's eyes for a minute.

Heart to Heart

At the next light, Karen's parents held hands and gazed briefly into each other's eyes. Mom said, "Hi." Dad warmly responded.

Then the light changed, and the race was back on. It may seem an insignificant event. But to those parents and their children, it was an important reconnection in a hectic world.

Do your children really know how much you care for your husband? Do they see you being kind to each other and showing affection for one another? One of the best gifts you can give your children is the knowledge that their parents love each other and are committed to each other. It models for them what God intended love to be.

Perhaps you are a single mother or widow. You can demonstrate God's love through the way you treat your friends, family, or strangers. Real life is full of frustrations, challenges, and disappointments—and our relationships with each other are no exception. Life is not perfect, but love is.

One way we love is through connecting, heart to heart, with other people. It is not enough to listen with our ears—we need to listen with our hearts as well. Proverbs 27:19 says, "As water reflects a face, so a man's heart reflects the man." When we see a person's heart, we truly see them.

Dear friend, take time today to reconnect with those you love. Gaze into their eyes. See their hearts—and their love.

HIS WORD

"Now that you have purified yourselves by obeying the truth so that you have sincere love for your brothers, love one another deeply, from the heart" (1 Peter 1:22).

MY PART

Reflect on the people you hold most dear. Take time today or this week to call, write, e-mail, or have lunch with one of these people. Go through your list. Make connecting a lifestyle. It will make for more meaningful relationships.

MY STUDY

Exodus 33:11; Psalm 25:14

Ron and Judy have retired. But not from spiritually influencing their grandchildren.

Every summer, they host a weeklong Kuzins Kamp for their grandchildren—no parents allowed! The children must be at least four years old and toilet-trained.

"One of the main objectives is to have a positive influence on our grandchildren," says Grampa Ron. "We want to reinforce the biblical truths they hear from their parents."

A Rewarding Experience

Character building and good manners are emphasized during Kamp. The children say they learn about loving one another and others. And in fun ways, they learn about sharing, kindness, and even obedience. God said in Deuteronomy 4:9, "Teach [My laws] to your children *and* to their children after them."

God does miraculous works not only to benefit the people at the moment, but also so that the glory of these works can be passed on from generation to generation. Exodus 10:1,2 says that God performed "miraculous signs...that you may tell your children and grandchildren...and that you may know that I am the Lord."

Perhaps you are a grandparent. Do you realize the important role that you play in the lives of your precious grandchildren? They respect you and look to you for guidance. Don't let this influential time in their lives pass you by—and it will go very quickly. Teach them about God's laws, but also about God's grace. Tell them of the miracles, big and not so big, that God has done in your life. In addition to telling them, show them with your actions how He lives in you today.

There's nothing like a grandparent! Spend time with your grandchildren. It's a rewarding life investment to them and to you!

HIS WORD

"Bring [your children] up in the training and instruction of the Lord" (Ephesians 6:5).

MY PART

How often do you see your grandchildren? Do you take an active interest in them and their lives? Have you told them the story of what God has done for you? Take time to connect with your grandchildren in a real and meaningful way.

MY STUDY

Psalm 128:1–4; Exodus 13:8–10

ricia felt helpless. She and Dan were exhausted, and they were only into the third month of graduate school. Family time with their two toddlers seemed to be a thing of the past.

Then one Sunday their pastor delivered a message that would change their course entirely. He urged his congregation to lay aside everyday tasks once a week for a day of rest. Use the time for spiritual growth, he suggested, for family activities, for restoration, for reading, and for spiritual refreshment.

Rest in the Lord

Dan and Tricia fully understood their freedom in Christ and were in no way bound to keep this observance. On the other hand, they were tired. Very tired. And they were convinced that God was trying to get their attention.

In biblical times, keeping the Sabbath was meant to be a delight, not a duty. Keeping it brought great rewards, rejuvenation, and joy!

They thought it would be difficult, but Dan and Tricia decided to make Sunday special. Here's what they did.

First, they began to plan ahead. Tricia found that taking some time Saturday evening to do the ironing and prepare the next day's dinner prevented Sunday morning chaos.

Second, they set aside time to focus on the Lord. Before going to church, they created a worshipful atmosphere by playing praise music on their stereo. After church, and after a leisurely meal, they enjoyed reading Christian books.

Third, they took time for each other. Sunday afternoons were often spent on a date. Dan and Tricia looked forward to an undistracted, unhurried time together.

Friend, if you've not done so already, ask the Lord for wisdom in how to spend your Sunday. Consider how your family might make that day a very special time. If making such a commitment is scary to you, just give it a try. Take time to rest in the Lord!

HIS WORD
"This is the day the Lord has made; let us rejoice and be glad in it" (Psalm 118:24).

MY PART
Reflect on your Sunday activities. Do you take time to enjoy your family and rest in the Lord? Make it a priority to plan ahead each week so that you can slow down. Then enjoy a peaceful, yet meaningful time of worship and restoration every week.

MY STUDY
Genesis 2:2,3; Matthew 11:28–30

David worked at a coffeehouse. Someone asked him to share the gospel with a young man sitting in the corner. David was happy to do so.

The young man's clothes hung like rags on his skinny frame. He was lapping up his tea like an animal. And he smelled awful.

But David sat next to him, and they began to talk.

Love the Unlovable

David learned that the young man had grown up on the streets as an orphan and was only recently released from jail. He was quite hostile. David prayed silently, "Lord, I really want to love this man, but I don't have it in me. Please help me."

Suddenly, the man began to cry. David wondered where the belligerence had gone. Finally the young man said, "I want to pray with you so I can become a Christian." So they prayed together.

Then David pulled off his own thick, warm sweater, folded it, and presented it as a gift, saying, "I'm giving this to you in the name of Jesus. I want you to know that God loves you, and so do I."

The young man beamed. Then he pulled off *his* tattered sweater and gave it to David, motioning for him to put it on. David prayed again—asking God to help him show love and acceptance by slipping on the young man's dirty, smelly sweater.

With that selfless act, David finally saw the young man as God had seen him all along. God had seen beneath his repulsive appearance to his deep hunger for the love of Jesus Christ. Like everyone who accepts Christ, he had been immediately transformed on the inside. He still had an odor. But inside, he'd become a new creation.

Love by faith those who may seem unlovable. Like the man with the smelly sweater, people are waiting to be warmed with God's love and forgiveness.

HIS WORD
"I tell you the truth, whatever you did for one of the least of these brothers of mine, you did for me" (Matthew 25:40).

MY PART
"Loving heavenly Father, You created each person on this planet. Help me to see them as You see them. Give me a tender heart for the lost and lonely. May I never pass up an opportunity to minister in Your Name. Amen."

MY STUDY
Psalm 91:14–16; Isaiah 41:17–20

DAY 60

Early in nursing school, Arlene's professor gave a quiz. She breezed through the questions with ease until she read the last one. It read, "What's the name of the woman who cleans the school?"

Surely this question is some kind of joke, she thought. Another student asked the professor if this question would count.

What Is Her Name?

"Absolutely," the professor answered. "In your careers, you'll meet many people. All are significant. They deserve your attention and care."

Arlene learned the cleaning lady's name: Dorothy. And she's remembered that lesson ever since.

Friend, God says in Genesis that *all* people are created in His image: "God created man in his own image, in the image of God he created him; male and female he created them" (Genesis 1:27). God cared enough about what He was creating that He made us in His own image. How marvelous!

If God cares so much about each person He uniquely created in His image, shouldn't we do the same?

Everyone is special, no matter what they look like, how they dress, or what they do for a living. Every day we encounter people in service positions, often very low-paying, thankless jobs. They work behind the scenes to make your life easier, cleaner, and more comfortable.

Show patience and compassion to the wait staff and sales people you encounter. Speak a kind word to the cleaning person at your school, church, office, or hotel. Let them know how valuable they are. Show them the dignity God gave to them. Through your kindness, they will see Christ in you. This will plant the seeds that may lead to their own personal relationship with Him. And, my dear friend, it will make you more like Christ.

HIS WORD

"As God's chosen people, holy and dearly loved, clothe yourselves with compassion, kindness, humility, gentleness and patience" (Colossians 3:12).

MY PART

How many people in service positions do you encounter each day? Probably quite a few. In your brief encounters, make it a point to connect with people. Call them by name. Look them in the eyes. As you treat them with the dignity they deserve, they will see Jesus in you.

MY STUDY

1 Samuel 12:22; Psalm 139:13–16

The Woman's Heart

Wives, submit to your husbands, as is fitting in the Lord. Husbands, love your wives and do not be harsh with them. Children, obey your parents in everything, for this pleases the Lord.

COLOSSIANS 3:18-20

Countless volumes have been written to help men and women understand the differences between them. Some of the differences are so obvious we smile, while some are much subtler. Our attitudes and actions reflect our basic beliefs about the roles and responsibilities that God has outlined in His word.

We should understand two important concepts from Colossians 3: voluntary submission and sacrificial love. What a difference these can make in our attitudes toward each other as husband and wife.

If we truly honor each other as individuals and demonstrate respect, most challenges in relationships can be eliminated. When we accept the guidelines in God's Word for the pattern of our lives, we will find fulfillment and satisfaction. The need to compete with men will be replaced with the desire to complement the men in our lives.

Jesus saw people as individuals, not as male and female. He spoke to the Samaritan woman at her point of need. He used words of acceptance and kindness, which opened her heart to God's love. She in turn brought everyone she knew—male and female—to Jesus. Her testimony led many others to believe in Him.

God's forgiveness touches the hearts of men and women and allows us to function in harmony with each other to bring honor and glory to Him.

DAY 61

What kind of influence are you on the man in your life?

One day the mayor of a city was walking down the street with his wife when they came upon a building under construction. A voice from several stories up called out to the mayor's wife, "Hi, Penny."

That's Power!

They stopped to chat with the construction worker, who they discovered was an old high-school flame of the mayor's wife.

As the couple continued walking down the street, the mayor commented to his wife, "You see, if you had married *him*, today you'd be a construction worker's wife."

Without hesitation Penny replied, "If I had married *him, he* would be the mayor of this city!"

Whether you're married to a mayor or a construction worker or you're single, God has uniquely equipped you to influence your world for Him.

Many women fail to see the opportunities all around them. They give in to their husband's identity—feeling, mistakenly, this is God's design for women. Instead, husbands and wives should help each other achieve their goals. It's okay to be ambitious for yourself and your husband. A woman can inspire her husband to great heights.

Recently, I heard a man say he wants his wife to be recognized as her own person, not just as his wife. I can appreciate that because Bill said that to me on our honeymoon. He has always encouraged me to fulfill my potential as a human being and, more importantly, as a child of God.

Being a helpmate to my husband is my first priority, and I find joy in that role. I haven't given up my sense of self and adopted Bill's life as my own.

I fully share Bill's achievements because I've had a part in all that he's done. I helped him just as he has helped me to achieve more than I thought possible.

I urge you to understand and appreciate the significant role God has given you. You can be a positive influence.

HIS WORD

"The Lord God said, 'It is not good for the man to be alone. I will make a helper suitable for him'" (Genesis 2:18).

MY PART

God has given women the power to help change the world. For thousands of years, women have changed the course of history by influencing others. Identify specific ways you can be a positive influence in the lives of people you know.

MY STUDY

Proverbs 31; Matthew 5:13–16

DAY 62

Read again the familiar and beautiful words on the subject of love, written by the apostle Paul in 1 Corinthians 13:4–7:

> Love is patient, love is kind. It does not envy, it does not boast, it is not proud. It is not rude, it is not self-seeking, it is not easily angered, it keeps no record of wrongs. Love does not delight in evil, but rejoices with the truth. It always protects, always trusts, always hopes, always perseveres.

Praying for Love

What a standard! Jesus Christ, through the power of the Holy Spirit, can give us the ability to live like that *every* moment of *every* day. That's true regardless of our circumstances, our personality, the pain we've endured, or how we were raised.

A friend of mine speaks freely about how much she hated her father. He was a well-respected attorney, but at home he was a tyrant. His rage made it difficult to trust him. He drank heavily every day. When he was in a drunken stupor, my friend would walk by him and feel absolute hatred toward him.

Then she became a Christian. For a few years, she continued to hate her dad. The distance between them grew and grew. Finally one day while reading her Bible, she came across this passage in 1 Corinthians. She was grieved to the point of tears when she compared the hate in her heart to the biblical definition of love.

God never said people would be lovable. But God's love is absolutely unconditional—no strings attached.

By faith, my friend began to ask the Lord to give her this kind of love for her dad. God answered that prayer. Within a very short time, her attitude toward her father started to change.

She began to think of creative ways to express her love for her dad. When she did, to her amazement, he'd respond. Eventually, their relationship improved dramatically.

By the time her dad died, he'd become a Christian.

HIS WORD

"Hatred stirs up dissension, but love covers over all wrongs" (Proverbs 10:12).

MY PART

Who are you thinking about right now? Someone unlovable in your life? Do the words of 1 Corinthians 13 sound a bit far-fetched for your situation? Ask God to give you His love for that person, and accept His love by faith. Through His power, no one is unlovable. It's time to start praying.

MY STUDY

Leviticus 19:18; Luke 6:27–36

Rob and Deborah planned their camping trip, and left on time with their twins. Everything went fine until late afternoon. Rob couldn't quite remember the exit to take off the freeway. "Where's the map, honey?" Deborah asked when she noticed the concerned look on his face. Rob had left it at home. "I'll recognize it when I see it," he said, driving on.

Husbands Need Respect

At 9 p.m., it was dark. The twins were asleep. Deborah noticed Rob looked miserable. She gently massaged his neck. "It's okay, honey. Let's get a motel room."

The next morning, Rob had no defensive walls to take down. Deborah had chosen to honor him, despite his mistake. Without prompting, he asked for directions, and they arrived at the campsite in time for lunch.

Most husbands agree on the importance of one thing they want from their wives: respect. Honor means esteeming the position and importance of a person even if his actions are not always honorable. Honor is a choice that is not always easy. Elevating another above ourselves feels unnatural. It involves at least two elements: deference and preference.

Deference expresses courtesy, respect, and humility. It implies a courteous yielding of one's own judgment or opinion to that of another. Deference is putting another person first.

Another way to honor our husbands is to show preference for them. Even if you have children to care for, make your husband a priority in your life. It will keep your relationship strong and close.

To honor is to make a choice that is often difficult. Deference and preference don't come easily. I'm not suggesting your husband is always right or that you become a doormat. That's not the point. It honors God to respect your husband. But when we understand honoring as a sign of character, not of compromise, we make a powerful statement to our husbands and to the world.

HIS WORD
"Be devoted to one another in brotherly love. Honor one another above yourselves" (Romans 12:10).

MY PART
Ask God to show you ways you can honor your husband, even when he doesn't deserve it. Whatever your unique situation, God can show you what to do. When you do it, you will be honored—by God Himself.

MY STUDY
Proverbs 22:4; Psalm 45:11

Mickey Mantle began playing baseball for the New York Yankees at age twenty. "When I came to the Yankees," Mickey said, "I'd hardly ever had a drink. My father wouldn't have stood for me getting drunk. But the following spring, Dad died of Hodgkin's disease. I was devastated, and that's when I started drinking. I guess alcohol helped me escape the pain of losing him."

Say It Now

Mickey's father played an important role in his life. He did everything he could to help Mickey become an outstanding baseball player.

Despite Mickey's growing problem with alcohol, his career soared. He won many awards and his name became synonymous with baseball. He retired in 1969, but his drinking continued. By the early 1990s, Mickey's body began showing the effects. His liver was failing. Finally, he asked for help.

Mickey went to the Betty Ford Center and made an important breakthrough. "I told the counselor I drank because of depression that came from feeling I'd never fulfilled my father's dreams. I had to write my father a letter and tell him how I felt about him. It only took me ten minutes, and I cried the whole time. I said I missed him, and I wish he could've lived to see that I did a lot better after my rookie season. I told him I had four boys. He died before my first son was born. And I told him I loved him. I would have been better off if I could have told him a long time ago."

Mickey, who died in 1995, was sober the last two years of his life. At his funeral, former teammate Bobby Richardson told about a recent conversation he had had with Mickey. Bobby told Mickey Jesus loved him and would forgive his sin. Mickey placed his faith in Christ, saying, "I am trusting Christ's death for me to take me to heaven."

Although Mickey made peace with his past in therapy, think how meaningful it would have been if his father has heard him say the words. "I love you" are wonderful words to hear.

HIS WORD
"Dear friends, let us love one another, for love comes from God. Everyone who loves has been born of God" (1 John 4:7).

MY PART
Have you told your father lately that you love him? Do you tell your family members what they mean to you? Don't hold back from saying, "I love you." Don't let it become a point of regret when it is too late to tell them in person.

MY STUDY
Hebrews 13:1; James 2:8

As Keith and his wife finished breakfast and got the children off to school, he could feel the tension mounting. He had offended his wife. They circled each other warily. Then she began talking. Her words were righteous and were born from her need for the truth and a well-deserved apology from her husband.

The Argument

Her husband had honed the art of winning an argument at any cost, especially when he was wrong. So Keith's mind clicked into action as his wife began to recite the details of his error in this matter. He prepared himself for his defense. But at that moment, God did something surprising. Keith was suddenly dumbstruck. No words spilled forth. He sat silently as she finished her speech. Then he watched her fall silent. She steadied herself for the verbal assault that he had well trained her to expect.

But this time, to the astonishment of both of them, the verbal assault did not come. Instead of Keith's argumentative tone, five words tumbled out of his mouth: "I'm sorry. I was wrong."

In that instant, he was transformed. Actually, they both were. He was no longer the picture of reason and control, driving his wife to distraction. She was no longer the competitor. Her countenance changed. The frown that seemed so firmly implanted on her beautiful face melted away. It was replaced first by confusion, and then by a look that silently communicated a flood of emotion. Her smile shouted from the rooftops: "You are the most wonderful man to me, for you love me more than your logic, your process, and your need to win."

God desires that we humble ourselves first before Him, and then in love toward one another. What a wonderful example Keith provided for people who love the Lord and each other and who are willing to humble themselves out of love for each other.

HIS WORD
"This is what the high and lofty One says—he who lives forever, whose name is holy: 'I live in a high and holy place, but also with him who is contrite and lowly in spirit, to revive the spirit of the lowly and to revive the heart of the contrite'" (Isaiah 57:15).

MY PART
Do you have a need to be right or in control that keeps you from saying, "I'm sorry. I was wrong"? Is there someone you've wronged to whom you need to say those powerful words? Pray about it, then do it. Be sure to add the three gracious words, "I love you."

MY STUDY
*Proverbs 8:13;
1 Peter 5:5,6*

Amal was just seventeen years old when her father died. His death left a big hole in her heart.

Although she was reared in a Middle Eastern country in a family with an Orthodox background, Amal knew nothing about putting her faith in Christ.

A Father Who Never Leaves

The enormous pain of her father's death caused Amal to reflect on this long-neglected faith and consider God in a new way. When she heard about some American missionary meetings to be held, she wanted to go. It was there that she learned about God's forgiveness and how to have a personal relationship with Him.

The Bible tells us in several places of God's commitment to always be with us. In Hebrews 13:5, He says, "Never will I leave you; never will I forsake you." This message was very powerful and meaningful to Amal. God is the only one we can count on to always be dependable.

Another meaningful discovery for Amal was that God is a "father to the fatherless" (Psalm 68:5).

Amal said, "I needed a father who wouldn't leave and wouldn't die." Right there in one of those meetings, Amal knelt to pray and place her faith in Christ.

"After I prayed the prayer asking God to be my father," she said, "nothing changed externally; but internally, I *knew*." What she knew was that she now had a Father who would always be there for her.

As she grew in her faith, God filled the emptiness in her heart. When Amal married, she and her husband became missionaries in their own country so they could share with others how they could come to personally know the Almighty Father. Because she was secure in her Father's love, she could pass His love on to others.

HIS WORD

"A father to the fatherless, a defender of widows, is God in his holy dwelling" (Psalm 68:5).

MY PART

Dear friend, what's missing in your life? Is there an emptiness in your heart? God is the answer. He will fill the void. He will make the difference. And He will never, never abandon you. He promises!

MY STUDY

Hebrews 13:5–8; Isaiah 63:16

When Dan's study door was closed, no one was to disturb him. But one day his son Steve barged in and sat down. Dan asked him what he wanted. His son said, "Nothing. I just want to be with you."

Father Worth Knowing

Later, Dan reflected on this incident and compared it to our relationship with God. "How often do we do that with God? So many of us barge into His presence and share with Him our shopping list for prayer requests, and then get up and leave. We fail to sit and just enjoy Him. We fail to become fascinated with Him, to adore Him, to admire Him."

Oh, friend, that's so true. Our loving heavenly Father wants us to enjoy being in His presence. Of course, we have the privilege of taking our needs and desires to Him, but we should also spend time just thanking Him for who He is.

One way to bring perspective to spending time with God is to make a list of all the things you want to talk with Him about. Prioritize your list based on the eternal significance. For example, if you are praying for a family member's salvation, make that a top priority. When you think about your list with eternity in mind, it quickly clarifies your true priorities.

When you have prayed through your list, stop and take some time to enjoy being with God—with no lists, no complaints—just *be* together. Your heavenly Father wants to spend time with you just as much as an earthly father wants to spend time with his children. The intimacy you will have with God will be priceless. And the perspective you gain in your life will be eternal.

HIS WORD
"Enter his gates with thanksgiving and his courts with praise; give thanks to him and praise his name. For the LORD is good and his love endures forever; his faithfulness continues through all generations" (Psalm 100:4,5).

MY PART
"Loving heavenly Father, thank You for the awesome privilege of allowing me to just be with You—to learn who You are, to feel Your comforting presence, to know Your infinite love. Thank You for Your Word, which you have given for my benefit and blessings. In Your holy name, amen."

MY STUDY
Revelation 3:20; 2 Corinthians 1:3

DAY 68

Louise lives in Holland. Her daughter, Karen, attended college in Italy where she met a young American man who was a Christian. He invited her to a Bible study. In their long discussions about God, he told her of God's love and forgiveness. Soon Karen placed her trust in Christ.

Authentic Witness

Louise didn't understand the change in her daughter and was afraid she was getting involved in a cult. Karen, despite her mother's misgivings, continued to share her newfound faith with her family. One by one, each family member came to trust in the Lord. Louise's heart was very hard, but eventually she too came to Christ. Louise said of herself, "I was the last to come. I had the hardest heart."

I love that story. A young man far from home shared his faith; then a whole family, in yet another country, trusted Christ.

It is impossible to describe the joy that comes when you are the person God allows to be the instrument to lead someone to a saving knowledge of His Son, Jesus.

Karen's mother expressed fear about her daughter's

newfound faith. That is not an unusual response to the zeal and exuberance of a new believer. But as Karen grew in her faith and lived out a Christlike example to her family, the change was evident.

The Bible tells us in 1 Peter 3:15, "Always be prepared to give an answer to everyone who asks you to give the reason for the hope that you have. But do this with gentleness and respect." The young man in this story lived this out and Karen's trust in Christ was the fruit. Karen lived this out and her entire family became believers. What greater reward could there be for a faithful witness than to see your family members come to Christ?

Enthusiasm is contagious, and an authentic changed life gives evidence of the Holy Spirit's power to meet the needs of anyone who will trust and obey Him.

Who can resist a contagious witness?

HIS WORD
"You will receive power when the Holy Spirit comes on you; and you will be my witnesses in Jerusalem, and in all Judea and Samaria, and to the ends of the earth" (Acts 1:8).

MY PART
Friend, make a difference in your world —share your faith enthusiastically with those around you, wherever you are. Be sensitive to the Holy Spirit's leading. And be ready to give the reason for your faith.

MY STUDY
1 Chronicles 16:8,9; Psalm 9:11

DAY 69

Young couples spend much time and much more money planning the perfect wedding day. They stand before family and friends and exchange vows made to God and each other. After enjoying the ceremony, they face the reality of marriage.

Choose Commitment

One newlywed recently said: "Although I was filled with joy during my wedding, from the moment I stepped out of the church, my disillusionment with married life started. The thought was planted that we'd probably get a divorce."

This was an ominous beginning, but by God's grace, after two years her marriage improved. At a marriage conference, God led her to reject divorce as an option. She *chose to commit* to her husband and their marriage for life. Acting on that commitment influenced daily decisions on how she would react to every situation involving her marriage. Once the commitment was made, her options were limited to solutions that would keep her marriage strong and healthy.

God feels so strongly against divorce that He says, "I hate divorce" (Malachi 2:16). Those are clear words from our Creator. But God doesn't just leave us on our own in our marriage. We can come to Him with any problem or struggle.

Asking God for the strength and wisdom to keep your commitment is the best way I know to ensure a life-long marriage. Choosing to eliminate the possibility of divorce gives you confidence to work through any disagreement no matter how deep your differences might be.

Friend, marriage requires commitment. If yours is in trouble, ask for help. Talk to a pastor or church counselor, or attend a marriage seminar such as Family Life. Don't consider divorce an option. Matthew 19:6 states, "What God has joined together, let man not separate." God will help you.

HIS WORD
"For this reason a man will leave his father and mother and be united to his wife, and they will become one flesh" (Genesis 2:24).

MY PART
Perhaps you have been divorced or know someone who has. God is forgiving. But part of repentance is starting fresh. Make a commitment to your marriage, and make Christ the center of it. Encourage others in theirs. Marriage is for life, and God will help it be a good one.

MY STUDY
Proverbs 2:6–15; Ephesians 5:22–33

Everyone loves words of appreciation, even the most modest people.

Becky's dad was about to have his seventieth birthday. There were no special plans. It was well known in the family that he didn't like a fuss.

But Becky was determined to honor him in a special way. So she wrote, and rewrote, a four-page tribute to her father.

Tribute to Dad

Not wanting to make her dad feel uncomfortable, Becky decided to have dinner at home. Maybe the privacy of home would be less uncomfortable for her dad than a restaurant. She prepared all her dad's favorite foods.

The evening arrived and the guests took their places at the table. Turning to her dad, she read her tribute. While Becky read the letter, her dad's eyes were fixed on her face. When she looked up at the conclusion of the letter, she saw glimmers of tears in his eyes. The hug was the real thanks, and she knew she had given him the right gift.

The apostle Paul regularly expressed his gratitude to and for the people he was addressing in his letters. "I thank my God every time I remember you" (Philippians 1:3). "We ought always to thank God for you, brothers, and rightly so" (1 Thessalonians 1:3). What an encouragement it must have been to receive those words!

Are you thankful for your father, even though he's not perfect? Have you told God what he means to you? Even if you have thanked God for him, it would be a wonderful gift if you expressed to him the great esteem in which you hold him.

Just like Becky's father, even the most humble and modest people appreciate kind words and gratitude from time to time. Whether it's your father or your mother, make it a point to express your sincere gratitude.

HIS WORD
"Honor your father and your mother, so that you may live long in the land the Lord your God is giving you" (Exodus 20:12).

MY PART
Friend, God says in His Word, honor your father. Fathers need to hear their children's appreciation—even the shyest and toughest of men. Think about your dad. Then write a tribute to him, telling him specifically the things you appreciate. It will honor him and please your heavenly Father.

MY STUDY
Romans 16:1–3; Psalm 106:1,2

We talk often about God's love, but how do we *know* that God loves us? What gives us the confidence? Is it a feeling? Is it based on favorable circumstances? Is it wishful thinking? Is there any way to know for sure?

God Loves You

I once heard Brennan Manning tell this story. One winter, he lived in a cave in the mountains of the Zaragosa Desert in Spain. For seven months he saw no one, never heard the sound of a human voice. Each Sunday morning, someone from the village below dropped off supplies at a designated spot.

Within the cave, a stone partition divided the chapel on the right from the living quarters on the left. A stone slab covered with potato sacks served as a bed. The other furniture was a rugged granite desk, a wooden chair, a Sterno stove, and a kerosene lamp. On the wall of the chapel hung a three-foot crucifix. He awoke each morning at 2:00 and went into the chapel for an hour.

One night during what began as a long and lonely hour of prayer, he sensed Jesus Christ saying to him,

"For love of you I left My Father's side. I came to you who ran from Me, fled from Me, who did not want to hear My name. For love of you I was covered with spit, punched, beaten, and affixed to the wood of the cross."

Brennan realized no man has ever loved him and no one ever could love him as Jesus does. He went out of the cave and shouted into the darkness, "Jesus, are You crazy? Are You out of Your mind to have loved me so much?"

God's love is neither sentimental nor some elusive dream. It is an objective reality, revealed to you and me in His Word and through the action He took on the cross when He died for our sin.

God loves you, my dear friend. Never doubt that.

HIS WORD

"For God so loved the world that he gave his one and only Son, that whoever believes in him shall not perish but have eternal life" (John 3:16).

MY PART

"Father in heaven, I confess there are times when I doubt Your love for me. Then I remember the cross. Only Your deep, tender, abiding love could have sent Your Son to a horrible death so I might live eternally. Thank You, Father, for Your infinite mercy and love. Amen."

MY STUDY

Psalm 52:8,9; Exodus 15:13

DAY 72

A dear friend heard a message about God's love taken from 1 Corinthians 13. She believed the truth in the message and sincerely wanted to demonstrate God's love. Then the truth blindsided her.

God's love is the same for *everyone*, and that didn't exclude her dad. God's love toward her dad was equally kind and patient, and it didn't take into account wrongs suffered.

Loving Dad

My friend thought, "If God loves my father just the way he is, who am I not to love him also?"

Right then, my friend decided to love her dad just the way he was. She knew she needed God's help so she prayed daily for God's kind of love for her dad.

As God provided the strength, she took steps to restore their broken relationship. Though her Dad never changed much, she did. The realization came to her one day that the miracle of God's love for us is most beautifully expressed when we give that love to others.

Have you ever had trouble loving someone because they did not reciprocate your love, or didn't do it in a way you wanted or expected? Jesus tells us in Mark

12:31 that the second greatest commandment is to "love your neighbor as yourself." So, loving others is a command from God Himself. It is not dependent on whether a person loves us in return.

Too often we place requirements and restrictions on our love. After all, it is easy to love someone who loves us. My friend, it is possible to express God's love to individuals without their response, and the only change we see may be what happens in our own hearts. But God will be pleased with our obedience.

If you have a difficult father (or other relative), love him the way he is, as God sees him. Your change in attitude will heal your hurting heart.

HIS WORD
"Dear children, let us not love with words or tongue but with actions and in truth" (1 John 3:18).

MY PART
Consider God's great love. Then consider His commandment to love others. Ask God to help you love that difficult-to-love person in your life. He will help you. It's His way.

MY STUDY
1 John 4:7–12;
1 Thessalonians 3:12

A woman I greatly admire, Edith Schaeffer, has written a book called *A Celebration of Marriage*. During her almost forty-nine-year marriage to Francis, she learned the importance of giving him three gifts: honor, creativity, and understanding.

Based on her principles, here are a few suggestions to help you rekindle the romance and renew the passion in your marriage.

Return to Romance

First, respect and *honor* your husband:

- Learn to say, "I'm sorry. Please forgive me." And mean it!
- Let your spouse overhear you complimenting him to someone else.
- Praise his successes.

Another factor that makes a marriage thrive is *creativity*. Try some of these ideas:

- Serve his favorite meal in the way he enjoys it most. Does he love breakfast in bed? A candlelight dinner? A picnic at the park?

- Take time to do with him or for him something he really loves, even if you'd rather be doing something else.

The third factor is *understanding*. This simply means listening. James advises, "Everyone should be quick to listen, slow to speak and slow to become angry" (1:19).

Here are some ways to become a good listener:

- Make time to sit down and be available when he has something on his mind.

- Let him talk about things *he* wants to talk about.

- Learn to ask good questions. Let him know he is your absolute priority.

- Pray for him and *with* him.

Give your spouse the gifts that God has given you. He doesn't wait for you to love Him. He loved you first. The more you understand His love, the more you'll love Him and others. Why not start with your husband?

HIS WORD

"Let each man of you [without exception] love his wife as …his very own self; and let the wife see that she respects and reverences her husband [that she notices him, regards him, honors him, prefers him, venerates, and esteems him; and that she defers to him, praises him, and loves and admires him exceedingly]" (Ephesians 5:33, Amplified).

MY PART

"Lord God, thank You for the gift of my precious husband, and for the role he plays in our family. Help me to be a loving wife who is sensitive to his needs. In Your wonderful name, amen."

MY STUDY

Song of Solomon 6:3; 1 Corinthians 13:4–7

Does your family have special traditions that are simple, yet meaningful? The "Daddy moment" has become one such tradition in Vicki's family. It is a great idea for any family in these busy times.

Here's how it came about. Vicki's husband, the daddy of her children, seemed a bit neglected. Even if he hadn't noticed it, Vicki felt she had been too busy to pay him the attention he deserved.

The Daddy Moment

Then she thought of having a "be-nice-to-daddy" moment. When this idea first came to her, she talked to the children about it, and they were excited to participate.

So one day when daddy walked in from work, things changed! Vicki spontaneously initiated a "be-nice-to-Daddy" moment. Their children, then ages 6 and 4, joined in enthusiastically.

They dropped their toys and activities, giggled and squealed, and ran to meet daddy. It was a simple celebration—foot rubs, shoulder rubs, a cool drink, and the newspaper. What a blessing it was to receive such heartfelt pampering! Daddy felt loved and respected.

The children, now teenagers, still enjoy expressing little acts of kindness to their father. Family mealtimes frequently are punctuated by laughs about some silly "Daddy moment" that didn't go quite as planned.

My friend, that is what families are for. You should not only share the tough times together, but also the good times, the fun times, the times that you will talk about and laugh about for years to come. Families are also a place to build each other up and make one another feel special. Vicki and the kids did that for her husband.

Special days are set aside to celebrate moms and dads, but the greatest joy a Christian family can share is the day-to-day blessing of living as a family who respects and appreciates each other.

HIS WORD
"Therefore encourage one another and build each other up, just as in fact you are doing" (1 Thessalonians 5:11).

MY PART
Dads with young children may feel neglected not just by their wife, but by the entire family. Family and school activities create a hectic pace. Be sure to take time to make your husband feel special, not just as a daddy and head of the house, but as a person.

MY STUDY
*Psalm 126:2;
Romans 14:19*

DAY 75

always take a promise seriously. That's especially true when it comes from God.

Did you know that the biblical commandment to honor your parents is the first command that comes with a promise? In Deuteronomy 5:16, God says,

> Honor your father and your mother...so that you may live long and that it may go well with you.

A Command with a Promise

I remember a kind man who got up early every Sunday morning to make pancakes for the family—so that mother could sleep in. That man was my father. Later after church, we took long afternoon walks together, we'd go to a swinging bridge, and I caught crawdads in the stream while my father fished.

With children of my own, I can only now fully appreciate how he sacrificed for his family. Dad worked hard to provide for us, but he always took time to play and make us feel special.

He wasn't perfect, but respecting Dad has always come naturally to me. Honoring him was not a chore.

I realize that this may not be your story. Perhaps your father was not a strong, loving, family man. But whether your relationship was wonderful or painful, the command is to honor him.

How do you show honor to your father? Let me offer a few practical ideas.

Tell him what you appreciate about him. Be specific. If he was a good provider, tell him so. If he's been faithful to your mother, tell him how important that is to you. Bring up favorite memories from growing up. Thank him for everything he did right. And tell him you love him.

Even if you have a difficult relationship with your father, you can still obey God's command to honor him. In your case, honoring him may start with forgiving him. Ask God to replace your bitterness and anger with compassion.

HIS WORD
"Listen to your father, who gave you life, and do not despise your mother when she is old"
(Proverbs 23:22).

MY PART
Honoring your father is a two-way blessing. It is a blessing to the parent who receives thanks for what he did right. And it's a blessing to the grown child who can grow old with nothing left unsaid. Honor your father today.

MY STUDY
Exodus 20:12; Matthew 15:3–9

Have you heard anyone recently share their excitement as they talked about their grandchildren? Or have you listened to a young man who has just discovered the woman he wants to marry? These people are so full of the joy in their relationships that they couldn't possibly keep quiet about it.

Overflowing

So our relationship with God can overflow as we share with others our hearts full of joy, love, and gratitude concerning what God has done for us.

As a new believer, I wanted to tell others about Christ, but I was afraid I couldn't do it well because I wasn't familiar with Scripture. I knew we were commanded in Scripture to share our faith; I just didn't know the rest of the story.

Then I read 1 John 1:3: "We proclaim to you what we have seen and heard, so that you also may have fellowship with us. And our fellowship is with the Father and with his Son, Jesus Christ." From that verse, I realized that all I had to do was share what I had "seen and heard"—what God had revealed to me to that point in my life. As I did, I found many people were looking for the answers I had found. Even though I didn't know a lot about the Bible, people were interested in what had happened to me.

Not everyone with whom you share your faith will respond positively. Only God can bring results. I have learned that whatever reasons may prevent a person from responding, my responsibility is clear: I simply must share Christ in the power of the Holy Spirit and leave the results to God. When I am obedient to Him, I experience overflowing joy.

DAY 77

In many homes across America, Father's Day is a happy time of expressing love. For others, though, it's a time of loneliness, even anger and disappointment.

You may have grown up in a happy home like I did, so obeying this command comes easy. But for many, honoring their father is a stretch. It's an act of obedience, because their memories aren't all good. In fact, some of them are downright painful.

No Regrets

Let me tell you about Dodie, a woman in her late twenties. When she was very young, her dad left her mother. Throughout her childhood, she was deeply angry and hurt.

During those impressionable years of innocence, he wasn't there to tuck her in or to sit her on his knee. During the scary and volatile teenage years, again he wasn't home to answer questions or to meet her friends. And when she began making decisions of her own, he wasn't there to give her counsel and affirmation.

For most of her life, her memory of "Dad" was that he was *gone*, and she resented him for it.

As an adult, Dodie decided to obey the command to honor her father, knowing that, as she does this, God will honor her. She deliberately reached out to him in love and forgiveness. Dodie chose to focus on what he did *right*, instead of what he did *wrong*.

When she treats him with respect, she hopes that he'll taste God's love and forgiveness and decide to give his life to Christ. That is called *honoring by faith*.

So, when God gave the command to honor your parents, do you think He knew about *your* father? Of course He did! He is giving you an opportunity to display His compassion in a difficult relationship.

HIS WORD
"Finally, all of you, live in harmony with one another; be sympathetic, love as brothers, be compassionate and humble" (1 Peter 3:8).

MY PART
When you prepare for Father's Day, let me urge you to obey God and honor your father by faith. You'll be so glad you did! Dodie and her father have a brand new healing friendship that's emerged from the ashes. It doesn't make the past right, but it sure makes the future a lot brighter.

MY STUDY
Matthew 5:44; Psalm 27:10

ey Bailey stood on the edge of the swimming pool. She was barely three feet tall and scared to death of deep water. But her father stood in the pool, coaxing her to jump in.

He said, "Jump in, Ney! I'll catch you."

Finally, Ney jumped. Her head went under and she came up sputtering and thrashing. Her father wasn't there. He had moved back in the water, hoping she would swim to him.

Faith Is Not a Feeling

Ney began to cry. "Daddy, you moved! You said you wouldn't!" Her father laughed and said, "Ney, you've gotten upset over nothing. You know I wouldn't let anything happen to you!"

That innocent experience had a *devastating* effect on Ney's tender young mind. She had trusted her father completely, and he had let her down.

Over the years her lack of trust evolved into anger. By the time she entered college, there was a deep rift between the two.

While away at school, Ney gave her life to Christ. Early in her walk with the Lord, she learned that faith is not a feeling. Faith is being willing to take God at His word. Faith means believing God and choosing to be obedient, regardless of emotions.

Ney knew the description of love in 1 Corinthians 13. "Love is patient, love is kind, love is not provoked." She realized that if God loved her father in this way, she must do that, too.

Ney decided to take God at His word and to love her father without regard for his performance.

The next weekend, Ney approached her father about all the bitterness she had held and asked for his forgiveness. Without reservation, he forgave her. From that time on, he was warmer and kinder than ever before.

A few years later, Ney's father died. She was so glad to be free of regrets about their relationship.

HIS WORD

"If you forgive men when they sin against you, your heavenly Father will also forgive you. But if you do not forgive men their sins, your Father will not forgive your sins" (Matthew 6:14,15).

MY PART

Are you nursing some old wounds? Maybe a member of the family has hurt you. Don't you think it's time you put those hard feelings to rest? Give them to the Lord. Then trust God to remove all of the turmoil and anger. As you act in obedience to Him, He surely will.

MY STUDY

Proverbs 10:12;
1 Peter 3:9

While in college, Cindy became a Christian. The closer she got to God, the more she wanted a closer relationship with her dad. Cindy knew it would only happen if she took the initiative.

Don was the kind of dad who had difficulty showing emotion. He worked long hours and, when at home, he didn't want to be disturbed. Cindy felt estranged from her father.

To Dad With Love

Cindy often made it a point to hug her dad. At the end of phone conversations, she'd always say, "I love you, Dad." The closest he ever got to reciprocating was "Me too."

Then it came time to move across the country to begin a new job. When she loaded up her car and waved good-bye to her family, Cindy didn't yet know the significance of this farewell.

A few weeks later, a fleeting thought popped into her mind. She should send her father a card. For most people, sending a card was no big deal. For Cindy, that wasn't the case. The only time she'd ever sent her father a card was on his birthday. But she knew she had to do this.

So she found a silly card and wrote a short note:

Hi Dad! Things are going well here. Just wanted to let you know I was thinking about you. I love you,

> Cindy

It didn't take much effort. It almost seemed insignificant. But not to Cindy's father. He was bowled over. For weeks, the card was almost all he talked about.

By her father's reaction, Cindy knew that fleeting thought was a prompting from God. It gave her the opportunity to very clearly let her father know how much she loved him.

One month after sending the card, Cindy's father died unexpectedly. Her farewell before leaving home was the last time she saw her dad. Yet she knew she'd left no words unspoken.

HIS WORD
"Be imitators of God, therefore, as dearly loved children and live a life of love, just as Christ loved us and gave himself up for us as a fragrant offering and sacrifice to God" (Ephesians 5:1,2).

MY PART
Friend, think about your relationships. Is there something you've left unsaid? Don't wait until it's too late. Do you need to write a letter or make a phone call? Maybe a visit would be appropriate. Let your loved ones know what they mean to you. If you do, you'll live with no regrets.

MY STUDY
Romans 13:7; Proverbs 3:27

DAY 80

In his book *Point Man*, Steve Farrar tells the fascinating story of George McCluskey.

When George McCluskey married and started a family, he made another commitment as well. He decided to invest one hour each day in prayer. His supreme desire was for his children to follow Christ.

Generations of Prayer

He prayed as they grew up, married, and had their own children. George then began praying for his grandchildren, too. In later years, he included his great-grandchildren in those faithful prayers. Every day, from eleven to noon, he prayed for all three generations.

George first saw his two daughters commit their lives to Christ. Each one married a man who went into the ministry.

Between the two couples, they had five children—four girls and one boy. Each one of his granddaughters married preachers, and his grandson became a pastor.

The first two children of the next generation—George's great-grandchildren—were boys. When those two young men graduated from high school, they went to the same college and were roommates.

During their sophomore year, one boy decided to go into the ministry. The other didn't. Instead, he had a growing interest in psychology.

Eventually, the young man earned a doctorate. After that, he began writing books on parenting, which almost immediately became best-sellers. Then he started a radio program. That program is now heard every day on hundreds of stations around the world.

If you haven't already guessed, the man is…Dr. James Dobson of Focus on the Family!

God graciously honored the consistent prayers of James Dobson's faithful great-grandfather! And God will do the same for you and me. Pray for your family regularly. It will affect them for generations to come.

HIS WORD
"If you believe, you will receive whatever you ask for in prayer" (Matthew 21:22).

MY PART
"Loving heavenly Father, that You hear my prayers and have compassion on me and my family is truly a source of peace and joy for me. Thank You for being a compassionate, merciful God whose love is everlasting. In Your mighty name, amen."

MY STUDY
Psalm 145:18; Luke 11:9

DAY 81

Rachel grew up in what she thought was a pretty normal home: a mom, a dad, a sister, a couple of brothers. A normal house on a normal street.

However, Rachel's parents argued privately. Year by year, there were more arguments on the other side of the house. They got louder and longer.

"Love One Another Deeply"

Rachel's dad was developing an alcohol addiction. He was a great guy when he was sober. But the minute he took a drink, even in private, his personality changed. He wasn't violent, just different. After a few drinks, he'd become obnoxious. Then he slept. Rachel *hated* his drinking. And like the arguments, his drinking was private.

By the time Rachel went off to college, things were really bad. Her dad was drinking a lot more and her parents' relationship had all but dissolved.

Rachel, who had trusted Jesus Christ as a youngster, was learning to walk with God. Now, God became her source of strength and comfort.

Soon after she came home from college, Rachel's dad learned he needed an operation. Through this difficult time, God was working in her heart.

Rachel stood at her dad's bedside in the hospital. She looked at him and silently prayed, "Lord, let me love Dad just the way he is, even if he drinks the rest of his life."

Rachel knew that God loved her just as she was. And she knew she needed to show her dad the same kind of love, so he would see Jesus in her.

God answered Rachel's prayer. She has loved her dad, no matter what, ever since. Yes, there were difficult times, but her love made them easier.

Today, her dad is sober. That wonderful personality she loves in her dad is back. And they share a good relationship.

HIS WORD

"Now that you have purified yourselves by obeying the truth so that you have a sincere love for your brothers, love one another deeply, from the heart" (1 Peter 1:22).

MY PART

We all have someone in our life who is difficult to love. Dear friend, who is that person in your life? Ask God to give you a sincere love for him or her as only He can do. He will love through you if you will let Him.

MY STUDY

Song of Songs 8:6; Ecclesiastes 7:9

It was Father's Day in a very busy, but quaint, French restaurant where Roger and Lori were enjoying their meal together. They were stealing a few quiet moments alone without their four small children.

At the table next to theirs, a harried father sat at a long table with his *five* little children. They were beautifully dressed. His serene wife sat at the other end.

You Never Know

Roger and Lori looked at each other and whispered, "Wow! They have five children! And they've brought them to a French bistro with linen tablecloths for Father's Day! That's brave!"

Throughout the meal, the children were up and down for various reasons, as children often are. At one time or another, each of the children spent a few moments on Dad's lap as he attempted to navigate a few bites of his own meal around their squiggly bodies.

It didn't seem like a relaxing Father's Day for this gentleman. The mother—who had an infant snuggled on her shoulder the entire time—seemed unaffected. She smiled her way through the whole experience.

Roger wondered how the father had managed all this. He must be independently wealthy, maybe a doctor. They looked like one big happy, busy family.

When their meal was done, Roger and Lori complimented the mother on such a beautiful family.

That's when they discovered the *real* story. It wasn't a husband and wife at the table. The woman at the table owned the restaurant, and the infant on her shoulder was her only child. She and her husband were treating this dear man and his four children to a fine meal at their restaurant because his wife was her dearest and best friend. Only a few weeks before, her best friend had been struck and killed by a car while crossing a busy intersection. The father's caring friends didn't want this precious family to go through Father's Day without lots of company and love.

Dear friend, that is what it means to love your neighbor as yourself.

HIS WORD

"We who are strong ought to bear with the failings of the weak and not please ourselves. Each of us should please his neighbor for his good, to build him up" (Romans 15:1,2).

MY PART

We must treat friends, neighbors, and strangers with compassion, asking God to help us know how to reach out to others with love and understanding. Only God knows the heart. Yet He's chosen us to be His instrument. Only He can give us wisdom and courage to reach out with grace.

MY STUDY

Psalm 86:15; Lamentations 3:22,23

isa, the wife of a U.S. senator, attended a Bible study every week. But she made it clear that her perfect attendance represented her curiosity, not her belief.

One day after the study, Sallie, who led the group, stopped to talk with Lisa. Sallie asked, "Lisa, what do you think about what you've been learning from the Bible?"

Talk About God

Lisa was quick to reply. She said, "Sallie, do you want to be my *friend* or just convert me?"

In her soft, gentle manner, Sallie told Lisa, "More than anything else in life, I want you to know Jesus. But if you never believe, Lisa, I'll still love you."

Every week Lisa would go home and tell her husband, the senator, all about the things she'd discovered in the Bible. Her husband did not know Jesus Christ either, but was curious.

The senator, like many of his colleagues, had gone to Washington with high hopes. But in time, he grew frustrated with the bureaucracy and became discouraged. He began looking for answers that weren't in Washington. He sensed they were in what his wife told him each week after her Bible study.

Then one day, Lisa called Sallie. She said, "Sallie, I think my husband wants to know God." So Sallie asked an associate to meet with the senator and to share the gospel with him.

One morning a few days later, Lisa reported that her husband had tossed and turned all night. He got up and went downstairs. "I think he beat me to it," she said. "I think he did what you've been wanting me to do." The senator had knelt alone in the night and trusted Jesus Christ.

He started a Bible study in his senate office and spoke openly of his faith.

God's Word is far-reaching—to places we never expected. Talk openly about your faith because you never know who's listening.

HIS WORD

"My word that goes out from my mouth . . . will not return to me empty, but will accomplish what I desire and achieve the purpose for which I sent it" (Isaiah 55:11).

MY PART

You don't need a special gift to be God's messenger! When you talk about God, others become interested. God will lead the way. He wants to use you to achieve His purposes. Talk about Him and His Word. He'll make the truth known.

MY STUDY

Matthew 28:18–20; Psalm 40:9,10

After a fun day fishing with a friend and her father, an eight-year-old demanded of her mother, "I want a dad." For the next few minutes, she and her six-year-old sister begged their mom to marry and give them a dad. They even began listing eligible men.

No Substitute

"The conversation pierced my heart like an arrow," wrote their mother, Sandy, a reporter for the *Los Angeles Times*. She continued, "I thought I'd built a nice life, a complete life, my girls and I, in the years since their father died. I thought I'd stepped ably into his shoes, filling the roles he'd played in their lives."

Sandy earns a comfortable income, providing well for her three daughters. She taught them to roller skate and ride bikes, and she takes them on hiking and camping trips. She even learned to play basketball so she could coach her oldest daughter's team.

But all she does to fill those empty shoes hasn't been enough to fill the empty spot in those three hearts. The girls want, and need, a daddy. He was the big guy who let them ride on his broad shoulders and snooze with him in front of the TV.

In one quick moment he was gone, and their lives changed forever. Sandy wrote, "The children have been shortchanged, their childhoods diminished by the loss of something that, for all my posturing, I can never replace."

Children need their daddy. There is *no* substitute. I don't know why God allowed these three girls to lose their daddy. It's all dreadfully tragic.

Many men and women today are thinking of getting a divorce and leaving their children. I can't imagine how painful that must be for little ones. You made a commitment in your marriage vows. God says those are not to be easily broken. Friend, God is a God of love, mercy, and grace. It grieves His heart to see broken relationships.

We can find hope in God, His Word, and His Spirit. Turn to Him today.

HIS WORD
"Commit to the Lord whatever you do, and your plans will succeed" (Proverbs 16:3).

MY PART
Turn to God and let Him heal your marriage, for the sake of your children and yourself. If your marriage is in trouble, I urge you to get help.

MY STUDY
*Psalm 71:1;
Proverbs 16:9*

Adoration" is the word Claire uses to describe her dad's love for her mother. And "total commitment" is how she describes her mother's love for her dad. Theirs is a great love, a love that's endured more than sixty years. Claire also had another model of love in the marriage of her husband's parents.

It Takes More Than Love

Following that legacy of love should have been easy, or so Claire thought. When Claire married, she assumed she'd have a similar marriage, strong and loving.

Children need deep, abiding love and godly commitment between their parents. But it isn't automatically passed on, and it wasn't passed on to Claire.

She loved her husband, and he loved her. But, friend, love, in and of itself, isn't enough to make a marriage work. She said, "My husband and I had to build our own relationship one day at a time."

The models of their parents' relationships gave them an example to follow. But Claire and her husband were individuals with many differences, likes and dislikes, hopes and dreams. They had to grow together. They had to develop their unique relationship, their own bond of love.

So they worked at their marriage, and they discovered one essential ingredient that made all the difference.

Claire describes it like this: "It was not until we began to go together, in faith, to God's Word for its guidelines and promises that our marriage really began to get a firm footing. That Word provided the solid rock we needed to build on."

Friend, it's never too late to turn to God. If you've never made Him a part of your marriage, start now. Your love for God and for each other will grow in ways you never imagined. He will help you build together on His foundation of love.

HIS WORD
"Everyone who hears these words of mine and puts them into practice is like a wise man who has built his house on the rock. The rain came down, the streams rose, and the winds blew and beat against that house; yet it did not fall, because it had its foundation on the rock" (Matthew 7:24,25).

MY PART
Tonight after the children are in bed, read Ephesians with your spouse. It's a wonderful place to begin to build a solid foundation for a stronger marriage. Remember, it takes more than love.

MY STUDY
Psalm 127:1; Isaiah 51:1

DAY 86

It had been twenty years since Travita Kenoly had renewed her commitment to Christ. Though she'd placed her faith in Christ some years earlier, she wasn't walking with God.

One day she chose to return to her faith, surrendering once again to Christ. When she did, she began praying for God to change her and her husband, Ron.

He Will Answer

Travita said, "As I saw changes in my life, I could pray for Ron." She asked a group of Christian friends to pray as well. They reassured her that God would answer their prayers. "However long it takes, Ron will come back to faith," they said.

God answered the prayers of those faithful women. Just a few months later, Ron returned to the faith in Christ that he too had once walked away from.

As the Kenolys began growing in their renewed faith, they began praying for their three sons. They wanted their lives to make a difference for Christ. "We tried to live an exemplary, godly life," Ron said.

Suddenly, their oldest son, Tony, who was sixteen, ran away from home. They were heartbroken. "It brought us to our knees, weeping, and wailing, and hurting," said Ron.

Tony was gone three years. Although they saw him occasionally, they never knew where he lived.

Once again, a group of women in their church prayed day and night, this time for Tony. God answered those prayers as well.

With great sadness and brokenness, Tony finally came home. "He realized how much he needed his family and how much we needed him," Ron said.

Gratefully, this story had a happy ending. But Travita said, "I still pray as intensely for my children. I don't want to get complacent, knowing that the enemy is always waiting."

Friend, the adage says, "Prayer changes things." I say, God changes things through prayer. The Kenolys are a perfect example.

HIS WORD

"In the morning, O LORD, you hear my voice; in the morning I lay my requests before you and wait in expectation" (Psalm 5:3).

MY PART

God is a God of love and mercy. His love is perfect every moment of every day. It never changes. Like a father, He's waiting with all of that love for you to return to Him. All you have to do is call out to Him. Remember, God answers prayer. Tell Him your greatest need today. Talk with Him every day. And watch for His answers.

MY STUDY

Luke 15:11–31; Psalm 51:10–12

DAY 87

On the outside, Becky's father was the picture of health. But on the inside, he had a dangerous heart condition. He needed extensive heart surgery.

After a long day of flights, Becky arrived at her dad's hospital bedside. He looked good. He was talking and visiting with other family members. Then Becky asked to pray with him. They all bowed their heads while she asked God to watch over her father.

Trusting God

Early the next morning, they all met in his room. Again, Becky led them in prayer.

Becky and her brother, Richard, walked alongside the gurney as he was wheeled through the hospital.

Richard said to Becky, "We may never see him again."

As their dad was wheeled away to an uncertain future, they watched until the closing doors blocked their view.

Seven long hours later, the word came that the operation was successful. But the doctor was having trouble getting him stabilized.

Soon it seemed alright, and they were allowed to

see him. He was unconscious, cold, and had needles and tubes everywhere, but still they talked and encouraged him—and Becky prayed.

Suddenly, his blood pressure dropped dangerously low.

Everyone was scared. Becky called family and friends all over the country and asked for prayer. As she paced the waiting room, she told God, "If you want to take Dad home, Lord, it's okay. But, truthfully, I'm not ready to lose him."

She gathered the family and led them in prayer again.

Later, the doctor said if things didn't improve in two hours, he'd have to go back to surgery. Tearfully, the family prayed again. And they waited.

The doctor returned after only one hour, this time with a *good* report. The bleeding had stopped. Several hours later, he was stable and on his way to a full recovery.

Dear friend, God hears and answers our prayers.

HIS WORD
"Then they cried to the Lord in their trouble, and he saved them from their distress" (Psalm 107:13).

MY PART
I have no idea what's troubling your heart today. Whatever it is, God knows. And He'll help you through this distressful time. When you talk with God, you're telling Him you trust Him. Today, tell Him what's on your heart. Tell Him you need His help. Show Him you trust Him. You'll be amazed at what He will do.

MY STUDY
Philippians 4:6,7; Joshua 1:9

Lisa was growing in her relationship with Christ. But as fast as she grew, her husband's relationship with God went on a downhill run.

He became absorbed in his work. His job demanded many business trips. There were times that he wasn't home to attend church with her.

Lisa was very concerned—and frustrated.

Stop Nagging, Start Praying

Lisa's story is told in Stormie Omartian's book *The Power of a Praying Wife*. Sadly, I don't think Lisa's story is all that uncommon.

Lisa longed to grow together with her husband in the spiritual dimension. She wanted it to be a lifelong shared experience, but that's not what was happening.

She occasionally spoke with her husband about the problem, but he would become defensive and blame it on his work. It wasn't long before his work became a greater challenge, causing him a lot of stress. In her heart, Lisa knew that if he would turn back to God, he would find the strength he needed.

At this point, Lisa knew he wasn't going to listen to her about it any longer. So she began praying every day that God would develop a desire in his heart for God to be more a part of his life.

She prayed consistently and fervently for months, with no change. Then to her surprise, one morning he said, "I'm going to the office earlier today because I need time alone with the Lord before I do anything else."

God answered her faithful prayers. For the past few years, he's gone in early on a regular basis to spend time with God. Lisa's husband is a changed man in many ways.

Many of us want another person to change, but we are powerless to change others. God isn't. It's His business to change people. And He will. I will say this strongly: stop nagging and start praying.

HIS WORD
"Evening, morning and noon I cry out in distress, and he hears my voice" (Psalm 55:17).

MY PART
Today, if there are changes you want to see in your husband's life, be careful. Ask God if there's a similar change He wants in your life. Invite God to make that change. Then, pray daily for the needs in your life and in your husband's life. God will change your heart and his.

MY STUDY
James 5:16; Proverbs 25:11

Ted was a senior in high school. Like many teenagers, what he wanted most for graduation was a car.

In anticipation of this milestone in his young life, Ted and his father spent a lot of time looking at cars. In fact, after months of searching, they'd found the perfect one, the one Ted was sure would be his graduation present.

Good Gifts from God

When Ted's graduation day arrived, he was excited. His youthful dream would soon come true. He'd have his own car, the one he wanted so badly.

That evening, Ted's dad handed him a package. It was gift-wrapped and about the size of a book. As Ted opened it, disappointment washed over his face. The gift was a Bible, and there were no car keys.

In a split second, Ted's disappointment turned to anger. He threw the Bible down and left the house in a rage. Tragically, the father and son never saw each other again.

Sometime later, Ted did go home, but it was after his father died. As he was going through some of his dad's things, Ted found the graduation Bible. He held it in his hands. Then he opened it.

There, tucked inside the pages, was a cashier's check. Yes, it was a check for a car. Dated the day of Ted's graduation, it was written for the exact amount of the "perfect car," the very one he and his father shopped for and found together.

This reminds me of the way people treat their heavenly Father. They pray for something. He answers differently than they expect. They're disappointed. Then they walk away from Him, even though God's answer always works out so much better. God promises to meet your needs. Maybe not in the way you expect, but He *will* do it. Trust Him.

HIS WORD

"If you, then, though you are evil, know how to give good gifts to your children, how much more will your Father in heaven give good gifts to those who ask him!" (Matthew 7:11).

MY PART

Write down one thing you need and one thing that's a desire deep in your heart. Put today's date on it and tape it inside your Bible. Then talk with God. Every day thank Him for the answer. It may not come exactly as you expect, but the answer will be perfect because He is perfect.

MY STUDY

Romans 8:14–17; 2 Corinthians 6:18

When Bill and I celebrated our fiftieth wedding anniversary, it was a time of joy and reflecting. Fifty years equals 18,250 days. Life is lived one day at a time and each day is a gift from God.

Looking back always allows a person to think of the things she might have done differently. I am so thankful that I have very few regrets.

True Devotion

There are wonderful qualities I appreciate about my husband, powerful principles I've learned about marriage, words of wisdom I could pass on to others.

But there is one thing, *one solitary* thing that has made our marriage strong and enjoyable. It has enabled us not only to *stay married*, but also to *keep* delight and joy in our marriage and keep our love growing.

That "secret" is that both my husband and I have an unbending devotion to Jesus Christ. He is our focus! As we've focused on Him individually for fifty years, He's brought us closer and closer together. We're much happier today than even the day we married. Our Lord gets the glory. We praise Him!

Devotion is the key to any lasting relationship. The closer we walk with the Lord, the closer we feel to each other. Our devotion for Christ has deepened through the years as has our devotion to each other.

Our culture today is on a fast track to everything! But we can't develop devotion on a fast track. Devotion is developed one day at a time as we submit to the leading of the Holy Spirit and allow Him to work in and through us.

The seasons of our lives demand varying amounts of emotional and physical energy, but our need for devotion to Jesus Christ is consistent. When we keep Christ first, all the other things take on proper perspective. Then when we look back, we can rejoice at what God has done.

HIS WORD

"Blessed is the man who does not walk in the counsel of the wicked or stand in the way of sinners or sit in the seat of mockers. But his delight is in the law of the LORD, and on his law he meditates day and night. He is like a tree planted by streams of water, which yields its fruit in season and whose leaf does not wither. Whatever he does prospers" (Psalm 1:1–3).

MY PART

"Lord Jesus, thank You for Your devotion to me. May Your Holy Spirit continue to guide me as I walk in the path of righteousness. I love You, Lord. Amen."

MY STUDY

Matthew 6:33; Deuteronomy 6:4–9

Beginning Your Journey of Joy

These four principles are essential in beginning a journey of joy.

One—God loves you and created you to know Him personally.

God's Love
"God so loved the world that He gave His one and only Son, that whoever believes in Him shall not perish but have eternal life" (John 3:16).

God's Plan
"Now this is eternal life: that they may know you, the only true God, and Jesus Christ, whom you have sent" (John 17:3).

What prevents us from knowing God personally?

Two—People are sinful and separated from God, so we cannot know Him personally or experience His love.

People are Sinful
"All have sinned and fall short of the glory of God" (Romans 3:23).

People were created to have fellowship with God; but, because of our own stubborn self-will, we chose to go our own independent way and fellowship with God was broken. This self-will, characterized by an attitude of active rebellion or passive indifference, is an evidence of what the Bible calls sin.

People are Separated

"The wages of sin is death" [spiritual separation from God] (Romans 6:23).

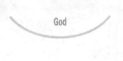

This diagram illustrates that God is holy and people are sinful. A great gulf separates the two. The arrows illustrate that people are continually trying to reach God and establish a personal relationship with Him through our own efforts, such as a good life, philosophy, or religion—but we inevitably fail.

The third principle explains the only way to bridge this gulf...

Three—Jesus Christ is God's only provision for our sin. Through Him alone we can know God personally and experience His love.

He Died In Our Place

"God demonstrates His own love toward us, in that while we were yet sinners, Christ died for us" (Romans 5:8).

He Rose from the Dead

"Christ died for our sins…He was buried…He was raised on the third day according to the Scriptures…He appeared to Peter, then to the twelve. After that He appeared to more than five hundred…" (1 Corinthians 15:3–6).

He Is the Only Way to God

"Jesus said to him, 'I am the way, and the truth, and the life; no one comes to the Father but through Me'" (John 14:6).

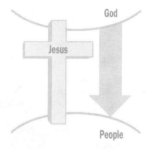

This diagram illustrates that God has bridged the gulf that separates us from Him by sending His Son, Jesus Christ, to die on the cross in our place to pay the penalty for our sins.

It is not enough just to know these three truths…

Four—*We must individually receive Jesus Christ as Savior and Lord; then we can know God personally and experience His love.*

We Must Receive Christ

"As many as received Him, to them He gave the right to become children of God, even to those who believe in His name" (John 1:12).

We Receive Christ Through Faith

"By grace you have been saved through faith; and that not of yourselves, it is the gift of God; not as a result of works that no one should boast" (Ephesians 2:8,9).

When We Receive Christ, We Experience a New Birth

(Read John 3:1–8.)

We Receive Christ By Personal Invitation

[Christ speaking] "Behold, I stand at the door and knock; if anyone hears My voice and opens the door, I will come in to him" (Revelation 3:20).

Receiving Christ involves turning to God from self (repentance) and trusting Christ to come into our lives to forgive us of our sins and to make us what He wants us to be. Just to agree intellectually that Jesus Christ is the Son of God and that He died on the cross for our sins is not enough. Nor is it enough to have an emotional experience. We receive Jesus Christ by faith, as an act of our will.

These two circles represent two kinds of lives:

Self-Directed Life
S – Self is on the throne
† – Christ is outside the life
● – Interests are directed by self, often resulting in discord and frustration

Christ-Directed Life
† – Christ is in the life and on the throne
S – Self is yielding to Christ
● – Interests are directed by Christ, resulting in harmony with God's plan

Which circle best represents your life?
Which circle would you like to have represent your life?

The following explains how you can receive Christ:

You Can Receive Christ Right Now by Faith Through Prayer
(*Prayer is talking with God*)

God knows your heart and is not so concerned with your words as He is with the attitude of your heart. The following is a suggested prayer:

> *Lord Jesus, I want to know You personally. Thank You for dying on the cross for my sins. I open the door of my life and receive You as my Savior and Lord. Thank You for forgiving my sins and giving me eternal life. Take control of the throne of my life. Make me the kind of person You want me to be.*

Does this prayer express the desire of your heart?

If it does, I invite you to pray this prayer right now, and Christ will come into your life, as He promised.

How to Know That Christ Is in Your Life
Did you receive Christ into your life? According to His promise in Revelation 3:20, where is Christ right now in relation to you? Christ said that He would come into your life. Would He mislead you? On what authority do you know that God has answered your prayer? (The trustworthiness of God Himself and His Word.)

The Bible Promises Eternal Life to All Who Receive Christ
"The witness is this, that God has given us eternal life, and this life is in His Son. He who has the Son has the life; he who does not have the Son of God does not have

the life. These things I have written to you who believe in the name of the Son of God, in order that you may know that you have eternal life" (1 John 5:11–13).

Thank God often that Christ is in your life and that He will never leave you (Hebrews 13:5). You can know on the basis of His promise that Christ lives in you and that you have eternal life from the very moment you invite Him in. He will not deceive you.

An important reminder...

Feelings Can Be Unreliable

You might have expectations about how you should feel after placing your trust in Christ. While feelings are important, they are unreliable indicators of your sincerity or the trustworthiness of God's promise. Our feelings change easily, but God's Word and His character remain constant. This illustration shows the relationship among **fact** (God and His Word), **faith** (our trust in God and His Word), and our **feelings**.

Fact: The chair is strong enough to support you.
Faith: You believe this chair will support you, so you sit in it.

Feeling: You may or may not feel comfortable in this chair, but it continues to support you.

The promise of God's Word, the Bible—not our feelings—is our authority. The Christian lives by faith (trust) in the trustworthiness of God Himself and His Word.

Now That You Have Entered Into a Personal Relationship With Christ

The moment you received Christ by faith, as an act of your will, many things happened, including the following:

- Christ came into your life (Revelation 3:20; Colossians 1:27).
- Your sins were forgiven (Colossians 1:14).
- You became a child of God (John 1:12).
- You received eternal life (John 5:24).
- You began the great adventure for which God created you (John 10:10; 2 Corinthians 5:17; 1 Thessalonians 5:18).

Can you think of anything more wonderful that could happen to you than entering into a personal relationship with Jesus Christ? Would you like to thank God in prayer right now for what He has done for you? By thanking God, you demonstrate your faith.

To enjoy your new relationship with God…

Suggestions for Christian Growth

Spiritual growth results from trusting Jesus Christ. "The righteous man shall live by faith" (Galatians 3:11). A life of faith will enable you to trust God increasingly with every detail of your life, and to practice the following:

G   *Go* to God in prayer daily (John 15:7).

R   *Read* God's Word daily (Acts 17:11); begin with the Gospel of John.

O   *Obey* God moment by moment (John 14:21).

W   *Witness* for Christ by your life and words (Matthew 4:19; John 15:8).

T   *Trust* God for every detail of your life (1 Peter 5:7).

H   *Holy Spirit*—allow Him to control and empower your daily life and witness (Galatians 5:16,17; Acts 1:8; Ephesians 5:18).

Fellowship in a Good Church

God's Word admonishes us not to forsake "the assembling of ourselves together" (Hebrews 10:25). Several logs burn brightly together, but put one aside on the cold hearth and the fire goes out. So it is with your relationship with other Christians. If you do not belong to a church, do not wait to be invited. Take the initiative; call the pastor of a nearby church where Christ is honored and His Word is preached. Start this week, and make plans to attend regularly.

Resources

My Heart in His Hands: Set Me Free Indeed.
Summer—a time of freedom. Are there bonds that keep you from God's best? With this devotional, a few moments daily can help you draw closer to the One who gives true freedom. This is the second of four in the devotional series. ISBN 1-56399-162-4

My Heart in His Hands: I Delight Greatly in My Lord. Do you stop to appreciate the blessings God has given you? Spend time delighting in God with book three in this devotional series. ISBN 1-56399-163-2

My Heart in His Hands: Lead Me in the Way Everlasting. We all need guidance, and God is the ultimate leader. These daily moments with God will help you to rely on His leadership. The final in the four-book devotional series. ISBN 1-56399-164-0

The Joy of Hospitality: Fun Ideas for Evangelistic Entertaining. Co-written with Barbara Ball, this practical book tells how to share your faith through hosting barbecues, coffees, holiday parties, and other events in your home. ISBN 1-56399-057-1

The Joy of Hospitality Cookbook. Filled with uplifting scriptures and quotations, this cookbook contains hundreds of delicious recipes, hospitality tips, sample menus, and family traditions that are sure to make your entertaining a memorable and eternal success. Co-written with Barbara Ball. ISBN 1-56399-077-6

The Greatest Lesson I've Ever Learned. In this treasury of inspiring, real-life experiences, twenty-three prominent women of faith share their "greatest lessons." Does God have faith- and character-building lessons for you in their rich, heart-warming stories? ISBN 1-56399-085-7

Beginning Your Journey of Joy. This adaptation of the *Four Spiritual Laws* speaks in the language of today's women and offers a slightly feminine approach to sharing God's love with your neighbors, friends, and family members. ISBN 1-56399-093-8

These and other fine products from *NewLife* Publications are available from your favorite bookseller or by calling (800) 235-7255 (within U.S.) or (407) 826-2145, or by visiting www.newlifepubs.com.